12-98

Enjoy cooking en Concert!

Best Wishes!

Joan Toole

Joan Toole's

Food for the Heart and Soul

The Art of Cooking En Concert

Acknowledgments

It is with a grateful heart and soul that I acknowledge the Peale Center For Christian Living, for their many years of continual inspiration. May the quotes in this book of the late Dr. Norman Vincent Peale continue to inspire and enrich lives as they have done for decades.

The quotes in this book are treasures that have been collected over many years from many different sources. If for any reason I have printed any quotes which should have had permission, I apologize and a correction will be made in subsequent editions.

Published by:
Eating In With Joan Toole® Consulting Services, Inc.

P.O. Box 937
Lake Forest, Illinois 60045
Telephone (847) 735-0036

Library of Congress Catalog Number: 97-90945
ISBN: 0-9659425-0-3
First Printing: 1998 10,000 copies

Edited, designed and manufactured by
Favorite Recipes® Press
an imprint of
FRP™
P.O. Box 305142, Nashville, Tennessee 37230
1-800-358-0560

Book Design: Starletta Polster
Art Director: Steve Newman
Editorial Manager: Mary Cummings
Project Leader: Elizabeth Miller

Cover Photography by: John Riley Photography

Table of Contents

Dedication

To my beloved husband and family,

my partner Tony Partipilo,

Kim Bradley and my ever faithful

"Dawn Patrol" running group.

Their encouragement, creative

suggestions and understanding

helped this book become a reality.

Thank you, thank you.

Introduction

Let's have better health, less stress, more laughter, more romance, more fun! As we wind down this millennium, restoring quality as a way of life takes top priority. After a long day put on the music provided by your CD. It will lift your spirits in minutes and soothe your soul while you are eating. By preparing your meal *en concert* you will discover a gift of more free time. Adopting some of the practical philosophy from the quotes under *Food for the Soul* will give you new inspiration. I guarantee you will feel better before you know it in all ways!

Cooking *en concert* with your cooktop, the microwave oven, the toaster oven and the barbecue is a great way to save all kinds of time in food preparation and still get the best of both worlds—delicious taste, quick preparation AND reduce kitchen cleanup by half. The *en concert* mixing of delicious fresh foods along with the prepared foods available today gives us menu versatility that was unheard of a mere decade ago and food in a flash!

In chapters 1, 2 and 3 there are complete menu suggestions with grocery lists included. "What's for dinner?" that familiar phrase, can be easily addressed by turning to the helpful tips contained in the "In the Pantry" section of Chapter 1. At the beginning of Chapter 2 you will find a "Great Variations" section suggesting simple changes to the recipes that gives a new taste and look to the foods featured, permitting multiple menu selections in moments. Cooking *en concert* will allow you to entertain elegantly with ease giving you time to enjoy friends and family. Chapter 3 shares menus, tips and assistance on entertaining elegantly with ease without losing a sophisticated atmosphere. The members of the organization Women for WineSense have selected all of the wine and food pairings, many times sharing tips on why they recommend that particular wine. Enjoy learning some important facts on the healthful side of moderate wine consumption. A glass of wine with dinner adds pleasure to even the simple meal.

But what about our attitudes? "Change your attitude and you can change your life," said the late Dr. Norman Vincent Peale. If we feed ourselves positive thoughts, we will ease our stress and soothe our souls. This helps us deal with the frustrations and challenges that come along on this road of life. The wisdom sprinkled throughout this book can nurture our souls and make life brighter and better. Adopt some of the philosophy suggested by wise people learned through generations of living. See if it doesn't add a positive dimension to your life as it has mine.

Food for the Heart and Soul will help you create a better quality lifestyle, with a gift of free time to use where you want and need it the most. *Food for the Heart and Soul* is dedicated to everyone yearning for less stress, striving for food for the heart and soul, and health for a lifetime! Enjoy!

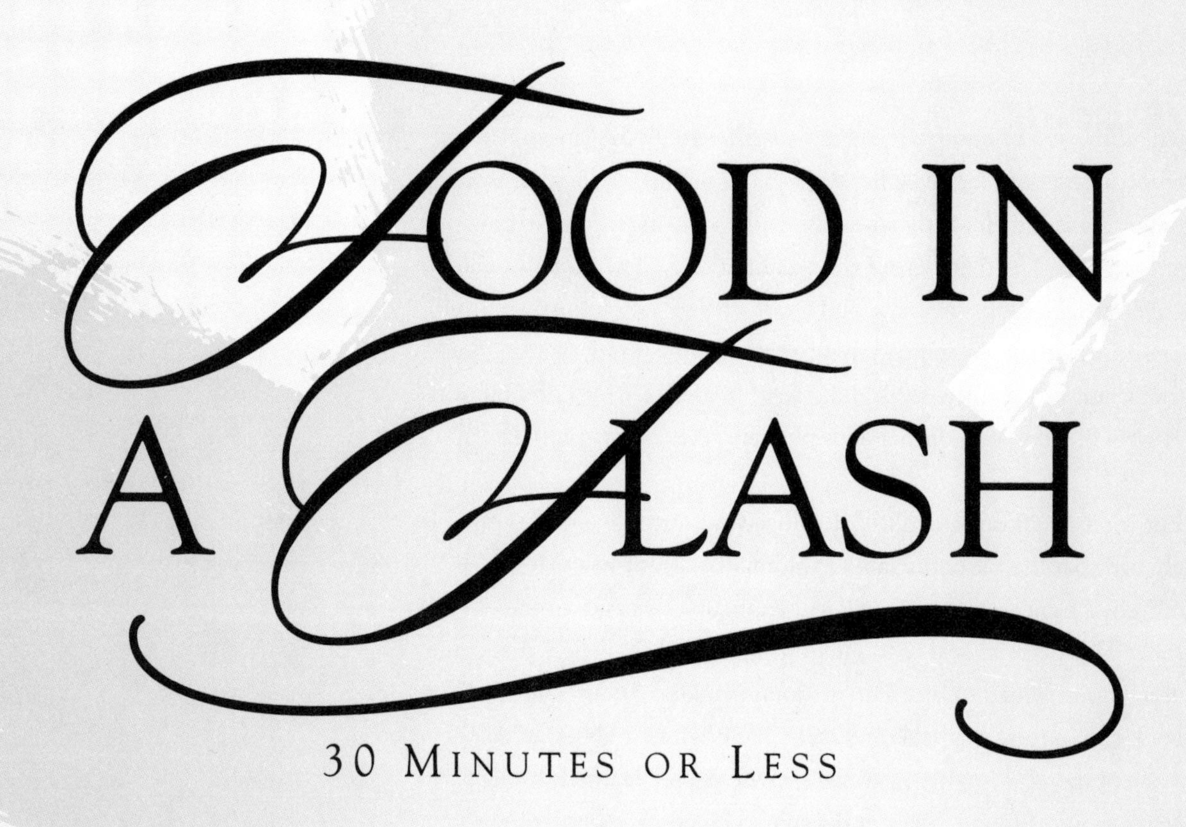

Food in a Flash

30 Minutes or Less

Menus

Fish Olé Dinner

Dilly Salmon Supper

Saucy Tilapia Delight

Dinner in a Flash

A Taste of the Orient

Sizzling Stir-Fry

Savory Skillet Supper

Heavenly Ham Feast

Pasta Magnifico

Home-Delivered Pizza

Porch Potato Pizazz

In the Pantry

The well-stocked pantry has expanded with the lifestyle of the 90s. Healthier products introduced in 1995 alone accounted for 12% of all new products presented. Take advantage of the abundance—stock your pantry! With these foods, preparation has become easier AND healthier. Having the following ingredients at your fingertips will allow you to create amazingly delicious and healthy meals in minutes from the pantry.

Staples

All-purpose flour
White and brown granulated sugar
Confectioners' sugar
Light pancake and waffle mix
Cornstarch
Baking powder

Spices and Flavorings

Dried parsley, tarragon and oregano
Dillweed, sweet basil
Poppy seeds
Onion, garlic and curry powder
Cinnamon
Chili seasoning
Salt and pepper
Vanilla and lemon extracts

Condiments

Molly McButter Seasoning or Butter Buds
Honey
Mustards (i.e., honey mustard, cranberry mustard, apricot mustard)
Canola oil
Low-fat prepared sauces
Low-fat or fat-free salad dressings (Strawberry Splash, Raspberry)
Low-fat or fat-free mayonnaise
Lemon juice
Favorite jams and jellies
Syrups (maple, berry)
Favorite meat sauces (A.1., catsup, etc.)
Low sodium teriyaki sauce
Soy sauce
Nonstick vegetable cooking spray

Canned or Dried Foods

Low-fat cream of mushroom soup
Low-fat cream of chicken soup
Beef and chicken broth
2 cans tomato paste
2 (8-ounce) cans tomato sauce
2 (8-ounce) cans spiced tomatoes
Dried cranberries, tart cherries and raisins
Cranberry sauce
Canned pineapple, applesauce
Favorite canned fruit (pears, peaches, etc.)

Cereals

- Low-fat or fat-free breakfast cereals
- Low-fat breakfast bars
- Oatmeal cereal packets or other favorite hot cereals
- Quick oatmeal

Dessert Fixings

- Pudding mixes (i.e., tapioca, vanilla, lemon, chocolate)
- Baking cocoa powder
- Light nondairy toppings
- Angel food cake mix
- Favorite cake mixes

Snacks

- Favorite low-fat baked chips and crackers
- Fat-free bean dip
- Low-fat dips, low-fat salsa
- Bagels
- Low-fat or fat-free cookies and brownies

In the Refrigerator/Freezer

- 50% fat-free butter
- Low-fat margarine
- Low-fat ham and turkey slices
- Egg substitute (i.e., Eggbeaters or Scramblers) instead of fresh eggs
- Low-fat or fat-free sour cream
- 1% fat cottage cheese
- Low-fat or nonfat cheeses (Cheddar, mozzarella)
- Low-fat frozen yogurt
- Low-fat yogurt ice cream
- Skim milk or 1% fat milk
- Prewashed salad greens
- Green, red and yellow bell peppers
- Carrots, celery, tomatoes
- Cucumbers
- Green onions
- Fresh fruit (cranberries, apples, bananas)
- Frozen vegetables (peas, corn, green beans)

Fast Food Fixings at Home

Simple and yet very healthy, these mixes are delicious and supper can be ready to eat in less than 15 minutes—right at home! New products that are good for you (low in fat—no more than 3 to 4 grams per serving, and high in carbohydrates, fiber and plenty of protein which satisfies our hunger) are being introduced all the time. Keep your eyes and ears alert for the latest and add them to your list. Simply add a tossed salad or a dish of fruit, such as pears and pineapple, applesauce, or peaches, some great bread, and it's done!

Supper Entrées

- Red beans and rice
- Noodle dinners
- Macaroni and cheese
- Instant mashed potato flakes
- Canned three-bean salad
- Baked beans
- Canned tuna in spring water
- Canned salmon
- White rice in easy-boil packets
- Dried noodles, spaghetti and fettuccini
- Fresh onions and potatoes
- Kasha and couscous

Condiments

- Extra-virgin olive oil
- Balsamic vinegar
- Raspberry vinegar
- Herbed vinegar
- Garlic

Utensils

- 1 large skillet (i.e., a well-seasoned iron skillet)
- Electric skillet
- Microwave-safe plastic dishes
- Microwave-safe glass cookware
- 2- and 4-cup glass measures
- 2-quart glass bowl

FISH OLÉ DINNER

FISH OLÉ

TASTY COTTAGE FRIES

MIXED CABBAGE SLAW

WHOLE WHEAT ROLLS

SERVES 4

DESSERT SUGGESTION:

Low-fat frozen yogurt with chocolate sprinkles

WINE SUGGESTION:

A fruity Sauvignon Blanc with a sassy herbal edge complements this menu.

EN CONCERT SEQUENCE:

Begin by micro-cooking the potatoes. While you are browning the potatoes, the fish will be cooking.

GROCERY LIST:

Groceries

2 pounds whitefish, orange roughy or scrod
1 (11-ounce) jar fat-free medium salsa
3 medium baking potatoes *
1 (16-ounce) package mixed cabbage coleslaw
1 (8-ounce) can pineapple tidbits *
6 whole wheat rolls

Staples

Garlic or onion seasoning
Nonstick vegetable cooking spray
Salt and pepper
Reduced-fat margarine
Fat-free mayonnaise

*Note: Staples are items that are usually found in the pantry—look before ordering. An * denotes items that could be considered staples for some families.*

Fish Olé

You'll enjoy fish in a flash with this recipe, and with all of its delicious flavor, you are doing yourself a nutritious favor, too. Relish!

2 pounds whitefish (orange roughy and scrod are delicious too)
1 (11-ounce) jar fat-free medium salsa

Method:

1. Place the fish in a shallow microwave-safe dish, arranging the pieces so that the thin end is tucked under and the thicker pieces are toward the outside edge. This allows the microwaves to penetrate more evenly.
2. Pour the salsa over the fish. Cover loosely with plastic wrap, venting one corner.
3. Microwave on High (100%) for 4 to 5 minutes per pound or until the fish flakes easily. Let stand, covered, for 5 minutes to complete the cooking process, then serve.

Approx Per Serving: Cal 329; Prot 45 g; Carbo 4 g; T Fat 14 g; 39% Calories from Fat; Chol 140 mg; Fiber 1 g; Sod 320 mg

Mixed Cabbage Slaw

We can thank the new prepared foods in the supermarkets for this simple and delicious salad. The crunchy, cold texture is the perfect complement to the tender, spicy fish.

1 (16-ounce) package mixed cabbage coleslaw
1 (8-ounce) can pineapple tidbits
3 tablespoons fat-free mayonnaise

Method:

1. Combine the coleslaw, undrained pineapple and mayonnaise in a salad bowl, tossing until well mixed.
2. Chill, covered, until serving time.

Approx Per Serving: Cal 80; Prot <1 g; Carbo 20 g; T Fat 0 g; 1% Calories from Fat; Chol 0 mg; Fiber <1 g; Sod 100 mg

THE FIRST CONDITION OF LASTING HAPPINESS IS THAT A LIFE SHOULD BE FULL OF PURPOSE, AIMING AT SOMETHING OUTSIDE OF SELF.

—Hugh Black

Life is an adventure in forgiveness.

—*Norman Cousins*

Throw off your "backpack" of anger and resentment today. You'll live more fully and feel 100% better!

Tasty Cottage Fries

This is the perfect recipe to enjoy the en concert *method of cooking—ready in less than twenty minutes from start to finish!*

3 baking potatoes
2 teaspoons reduced-fat margarine
2 tablespoons garlic or onion seasoning
Salt and pepper to taste

En Concert Method:

1. Wash the potatoes and pierce several times with a fork. Place on a microwave-safe rack or on paper towels.
2. Microwave on High (100%) for 6 to 8 minutes, turning once. Potatoes will still be a bit firm. Remove from the microwave with a hot pad. Slice into 1/4-inch rounds.
3. Preheat a heavy skillet over medium-high heat. Spray with nonstick vegetable cooking spray.
4. Add the potatoes and margarine. Sprinkle with garlic seasoning, salt and pepper. Cook until golden brown, turning frequently.
5. Turn off the heat. Let stand, covered, until ready to serve.

Approx Per Serving: Cal 124; Prot 3 g; Carbo 26 g; T Fat 1 g; 9% Calories from Fat; Chol 0 mg; Fiber 3 g; Sod 30 mg

Whole Wheat Rolls

Since microwaved foods heat from the inside, the rolls will feel only slightly warm on the outside, but will be warmer on the inside.

6 whole wheat rolls
2 tablespoons reduced-fat margarine

Method:

1. Split the rolls into halves. Spread with the margarine.
2. Place in a nonrecycled brown paper bag and sprinkle with a small amount of water.
3. Microwave on High (100%) for 25 seconds. Serve immediately.

Approx Per Serving: Cal 143; Prot 4 g; Carbo 22 g; T Fat 6 g; 33% Calories from Fat; Chol 0 mg; Fiber 3 g; Sod 268 mg

DILLED SALMON FILLETS

HERBED RICE

GREEN BEANS AMANDINE

APRICOT 'N CHERRY TOMATO TOSSED SALAD

SERVES 4

DESSERT SUGGESTION:

Strawberry-Tapioca Swirl (page 150)

WINE SUGGESTION:

A bright, tangy Sauvignon Blanc has enough acidity to perfectly complement the salmon and will blend beautifully with the dill seasoning.

EN CONCERT:

Cook the rice conventionally on the cooktop while you micro-cook the salmon and the green beans.

GROCERY LIST:

Groceries

1 pound salmon fillets
Fresh dillweed
1 (16-ounce) can French-style green beans, or
  1 (10-ounce) package frozen French-style green beans
1 (4-ounce) package blanched slivered almonds
1 head butter lettuce
1 head romaine or other lettuce
1 pint cherry tomatoes
1 purple onion
1 (6-ounce) package dried apricots
1 cucumber
1 bottle Silver Palate Good Old Apricot Mustard Sauce
Nasturtiums, geraniums, pansies or other edible flowers

Staples

Dried dillweed, parsley, tarragon, thyme, oregano
Lemon juice
Salt and pepper
Long grain white rice
Chicken bouillon cubes or granules
Reduced-fat margarine
1 bottle fat-free Italian salad dressing

Note: Staples are items that are usually found in the pantry—look before ordering.

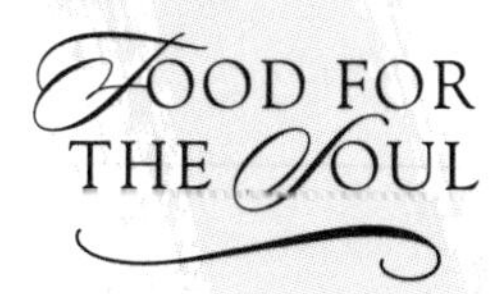

IT DOESN'T PAY TO BE TOO SENSITIVE OF SOUL. ALL OF US COULD TAKE A LESSON FROM THE WEATHER—IT PAYS NO ATTENTION TO CRITICISM!

North DeKalb Kiwanis Club Beacon

DILLED SALMON FILLETS

An elegant entrée, boasting the very good-for-us Omega 3 fatty acids.

1 pound fresh salmon fillets
2 tablespoons lemon juice
2 tablespoons chopped fresh dillweed, or 2 teaspoons dried dillweed
1/8 teaspoon pepper

MICROWAVE METHOD:

1. Place the salmon fillets in a 7x11-inch microwave-safe dish.
2. Sprinkle with lemon juice, dillweed and pepper. Cover with plastic wrap, venting one corner.
3. Microwave on High (100%) for 5 to 6 minutes or until the fish flakes easily.
4. Let stand, covered, for 5 minutes to complete the cooking process. Serve immediately.

CONVENTIONAL METHOD:

1. Preheat the broiler.
2. Place the salmon on a foil-lined rack in broiler pan, leaving space between the fillets.
3. Broil 5 inches from the heat source for 4 minutes.
4. Sprinkle with lemon juice, dillweed and pepper.
5. Broil for 4 to 6 minutes longer or until the fish flakes easily.
6. Cover with foil to keep warm until ready to serve.

Approx Per Serving: Cal 171; Prot 21 g; Carbo 1 g; T Fat 9 g; 47% Calories from Fat; Chol 68 mg; Fiber <1 g; Sod 52 mg

Green Beans Amandine

String beans date back to ancient Roman times. No strings attached these days. Beans are high in fiber and have no fat. Toasted almonds are added for crunch.

2 tablespoons slivered almonds
1 (16-ounce) can French-style green beans, partially drained, or 1 (10-ounce) package frozen French-style green beans
1/2 teaspoon reduced-fat margarine

Microwave Method:

1. Place the almonds in a shallow microwave-safe dish.
2. Microwave on High (100%) for 3 to 3 1/2 minutes or until golden brown, stirring once.
3. Place the green beans in a 1-quart microwave-safe glass dish. Add the almonds and margarine. Cover with plastic wrap, venting one corner.
4. Microwave on High (100%) for 3 1/2 minutes. Stir once and serve.

Conventional Method:

1. Place the almonds on a baking sheet. Toast at 350 degrees for 2 to 3 minutes or until golden brown.
2. Place the green beans in a 1-quart saucepan.
3. Add the almonds and margarine.
4. Cook over medium-high heat for 3 to 4 minutes or until heated through. Stir and serve immediately.

Approx Per Serving: Cal 65; Prot 3 g; Carbo 6 g; T Fat 4 g; 49% Calories from Fat; Chol 1 mg; Fiber 3 g; Sod 301 mg

Tip: *If using frozen green beans, microwave on High (100%) for 6 minutes.*

Everyone has a talent. What is rare is the courage to follow the talent. Life is 10% what you make it, 90% how you take it. Every person, every situation, can add to your success. Be yourself. Who else is better qualified?

START THE DAY
BEING THANKFUL!
DON'T DWELL ON
THE 3L'S, LACK,
LOSS AND
LIMITATION,
THINK POSITIVELY.

—Norman Vincent Peale

HERBED RICE

Rice is sometimes called the food of the ages. We know it is the answer for this day and age: high in fiber, low in fat, and delicious too.

To add a little kick to your rice, mix in some herbs, such as tarragon, thyme and oregano, and give your rice some extra pizazz. For other variations of herbed rice, see page 27 or page 57.

APRICOT 'N CHERRY TOMATO TOSSED SALAD

The sweet and sour flavor of the dressing adds zest to the mixed greens. The edible flowers are not only visually attractive—they taste good too!

1 head butter lettuce
4 leaves romaine or other lettuce
4 cherry tomatoes, sliced
1/4 purple onion, thinly sliced
3 dried apricots, chopped
1/2 cucumber, thinly sliced
1/4 cup Silver Palate Good Old Apricot Mustard Sauce
1/2 cup fat-free Italian salad dressing

METHOD:

1. Tear the lettuce into bite-size pieces. Combine with the tomatoes, onion, apricots and cucumber in a salad bowl.
2. Mix the Apricot Mustard Sauce and the Italian dressing in a 2-cup glass measure.
3. Pour over the salad mixture, tossing to coat. Garnish with nasturtiums, geraniums, pansies or other edible flowers. Serve immediately.

Approx Per Serving: Cal 59; Prot 1 g; Carbo 10 g; T Fat 2 g; 32% Calories from Fat; Chol 0 mg; Fiber 2 g; Sod 529 mg

Tip: *To save time, buy premixed salad greens, available in the supermarket produce section. Chill the remaining salad dressing in a glass jar; shake well before reusing.*

SAUCY ALMOND TILAPIA WITH CRANBERRY-MUSTARD SAUCE

LONG GRAIN AND WILD RICE

ZUCCHINI STICKS

SLICED TOMATO, CILANTRO AND PURPLE ONION SALAD

CRUSTY HERB ROLLS

SERVES 4

DESSERT SUGGESTION:

Pineapple-orange sorbet

WINE SUGGESTION:

Sauvignon Blanc, Chenin Blanc, Sancerre, Pinot Gris, or Riesling will all complement the fish.

EN CONCERT:

Cook the rice on the cooktop while you micro-cook the Tilapia and the Zucchini Sticks.

GROCERY LIST:

Groceries

- 4 tilapia fillets (about 1 1/4 pounds)
- 1 (10-ounce) jar 100% fruit cranberry sauce
- 1 (6-ounce) jar Dijon mustard
- 1 bunch fresh parsley
- 1 bunch fresh cilantro
- 4 ounces sliced almonds
- 1 (4-ounce) package boil-in-bag long grain and wild rice
- 4 small zucchini
- 1 purple onion
- 2 to 3 medium tomatoes
- 6 French rolls

Staples

- Reduced-fat margarine
- Nonstick vegetable cooking spray
- Dried cilantro
- Dried sweet basil
- Dried oregano
- Garlic powder
- Salt and pepper
- Balsamic vinegar
- Extra-virgin olive oil
- Confectioners' sugar

Note: Staples are items that are usually found in the pantry—look before ordering.

Think positively about your future! Throughout your day, make affirmations about your future. Say to yourself in the morning: "Things are going to be better for me today. I am going to think right and do right." Believe that God is helping you to move forward, and to develop and formulate a great future.

—*Norman Vincent Peale*

Saucy Almond Tilapia with Cranberry-Mustard Sauce

Tilapia has a smooth, velvety texture and mild flavor. I first became aware of this delicious fish on a tour of Eastern Maryland University's Aquaculture farms. A favorite for its versatility, I think you'll find the Cranberry-Mustard Sauce adds zip and the toasted almonds add crunch. A satisfying entrée ready in a jiffy.

1/4 cup sliced almonds
4 tilapia fillets (about 1 1/4 pounds)
1/4 cup Cranberry-Mustard Sauce (see below)*

Microwave Method:

1. Spread the almonds evenly in a glass pie plate. Microwave on High (100%) for 3 to 5 minutes or until golden brown.
2. Arrange the tilapia in a rectangular microwave-safe dish, tucking under the thin ends and leaving a space between the fillets.
3. Spread the Cranberry-Mustard Sauce evenly over the fillets. Cover with plastic wrap, venting one corner.
4. Microwave on High (100%) for 4 to 6 minutes (3 to 4 minutes per pound) or until the fish flakes easily.
5. Sprinkle with the almonds. Let stand, covered, for 5 minutes to complete the cooking process. Garnish with parsley and serve.

Conventional Method:

1. Place the almonds on a baking sheet. Bake at 350 degrees until the almonds are toasted.
2. Preheat the broiler for 2 minutes.
3. Arrange the fillets on a foil-lined rack in broiler pan. Spread with Cranberry-Mustard Sauce and sprinkle with toasted almonds.
4. Broil for 5 to 8 minutes or until the fish flakes easily.

Approx Per Serving: Cal 190; Prot 25 g; Carbo 11 g; T Fat 5 g; 23% Calories from Fat; Chol 67 mg; Fiber 1 g; Sod 127 mg

*For the **Cranberry-Mustard Sauce** combine one 10-ounce jar 100% fruit cranberry sauce and 1 tablespoon Dijon mustard in a small bowl and mix well. Store the sauce in a covered container in the refrigerator.

Sliced Tomato, Cilantro and Purple Onion Salad

This salad has a little bite to it that makes it especially good with the softer texture and gentle taste of fish, such as tilapia, sole, and whitefish. It also complements and adds color, with a good flavor difference, when served with steak.

2 to 3 medium tomatoes
1/2 medium purple onion, thinly sliced
3 tablespoons freshly chopped cilantro, or 1 teaspoon dried cilantro
1/4 cup balsamic vinegar
2 teaspoons confectioners' sugar
1 tablespoon extra-virgin olive oil

Method:

1. Bring 2 to 3 cups of water to a boil in a 1-quart saucepan. Blanch the tomatoes 1 at a time in the water for 30 seconds. Peel and discard the skin; slice thinly. Arrange on a crystal or pottery plate. Layer with the onion and cilantro.
2. Shake the vinegar, confectioners' sugar and olive oil together in a covered container. Drizzle over the layers. Let stand for several minutes before serving.

Approx Per Serving: Cal 73; Prot 1 g; Carbo 10 g; T Fat 4 g; 43% Calories from Fat; Chol 0 mg; Fiber 1 g; Sod 13 mg

Long Grain and Wild Rice

Why bother cooking from scratch when this tasty rice is ready in a mere ten minutes! The perfect partner with the velvety texture of the fish.

1 (4-ounce) package boil-in-bag long grain and wild rice
1 1/2 teaspoons reduced-fat margarine

Method:

1. Cook the rice using package directions, adding only 1 1/2 teaspoons margarine.
2. Stir to fluff, then serve immediately.

Approx Per Serving: Cal 104; Prot 3 g; Carbo 21 g; T Fat 1 g; 8% Calories from Fat; Chol 0 mg; Fiber 1 g; Sod 16 mg

Praise God,
we are free!
Freedom is
much more than
the absence
of physical
limitations.
To be truly free,
we must be free
of limitations
in our minds—
the gateway
to freedom.

—Daily Word

FIND A FEW MINUTES EACH DAY TO CONCENTRATE ON YOUR HAPPY THOUGHTS, AND SOON THEY'LL BE EASY TO FIND!

ZUCCHINI STICKS

The North American Indians called squash "askutasquash." Zucchini is one of the most versatile of the squash family. Try this to add flavor and nutrition in mere minutes.

4 small zucchini, quartered lengthwise, then halved
2 teaspoons water
1 teaspoon reduced-fat margarine
1/2 teaspoon each garlic powder and crushed dried sweet basil
Salt and pepper to taste

MICROWAVE METHOD:

1. Place the zucchini in a 1-quart microwave-safe dish. Sprinkle with 2 teaspoons water.
2. Combine the margarine, garlic powder, basil, salt and pepper in a small glass dish. Microwave on High (100%) for 30 to 45 seconds or until the butter is melted. Drizzle over the zucchini.
3. Cover with plastic wrap, venting one corner. Microwave on High (100%) for 4 to 6 minutes or until tender-crisp.

CONVENTIONAL METHOD:

1. Spray a large skillet with nonstick vegetable cooking spray. Add 1/4 cup water. Bring to a boil. Add the zucchini sticks. Cook over medium heat for 6 to 8 minutes or just until tender; drain well.
2. Add the margarine, garlic powder, basil, salt and pepper; mix well.
3. Simmer over low heat for 2 to 3 minutes or until slightly crisp.

Approx Per Serving: Cal 25; Prot 2 g; Carbo 4 g; T Fat 1 g; 20% Calories from Fat; Chol 0 mg; Fiber 2 g; Sod 10 mg

CRUSTY HERB ROLLS

The secret to enjoying bread without butter is to add a few tasty herbs. Try this recipe. Combine 1 teaspoon garlic powder and 1/2 teaspoon dried oregano on a sheet of waxed paper. Spray 6 French rolls with nonstick vegetable cooking spray and roll each in the herb mixture. Place on a foil-lined baking pan and bake at 425 degrees for 6 to 8 minutes or until browned and heated through.

Approx Per Serving: Cal 150; Prot 6 g; Carbo 29 g; T Fat 2 g; 9% Calories from Fat; Chol 0 mg; Fiber 2 g; Sod 345 mg

FAUX FRIED CHICKEN

HORSERADISH-FLAVORED MASHED POTATOES

GREEN PEAS

MANDARIN ORANGE-PEAR SALAD

POTATO ROLLS

SERVES 4

DESSERT SUGGESTION:

Fresh Peach Melba (page 146)

WINE SUGGESTION:

A fruity wine will complement this quickie menu. Select a Gewürztraminer, Riesling, or a dry Chardonnay.

EN CONCERT:

Begin with the chicken and while the chicken is cooking micro-cook the mashed potatoes then the green peas.

GROCERY LIST:

Groceries

- 8 skinless chicken breast fillets (1½ to 2 pounds)
- Seasoned bread crumbs *
- Instant potato flakes *
- 1 (8-ounce) carton light sour cream *
- 1 (5-ounce) jar prepared horseradish *
- 1 quart skim milk *
- 1 (10-ounce) package frozen green peas (without butter sauce)
- 1 (16-ounce) can pear halves *
- 1 (11-ounce) can mandarin oranges *
- 1 head lettuce *
- 8 potato rolls

Staples

- Salt and coarsely ground pepper
- Olive oil
- Nonstick vegetable cooking spray
- Butter seasoning (i.e., Molly McButter)
- Heavy-duty plastic food storage bags

*Note: Staples are items that are usually found in the pantry—look before ordering. An * denotes items that could be considered staples for some families.*

LIFE'S BLOWS CANNOT BREAK A PERSON WHOSE SPIRIT IS WARMED AT THE FIRE OF ENTHUSIASM.

—*Peale Center Plus Magazine*

FAUX FRIED CHICKEN

Crispy, quick, tender, and easy as 1, 2, 3, this chicken can satisfy your hunger for "good ole" fried chicken without the guilt. Enjoy!

8 skinless chicken breast fillets ($1\frac{1}{2}$ to 2 pounds)
$\frac{1}{2}$ cup seasoned bread crumbs
1 tablespoon olive oil

METHOD:

1. Rinse the chicken and pat dry. Place in a plastic bag with the bread crumbs, shaking to coat.
2. Preheat a heavy skillet over medium-high heat. Spray with nonstick vegetable cooking spray. Add the olive oil.
3. Cook the chicken 4 pieces at a time in prepared skillet until brown on both sides, turning once. Reduce heat to low.
4. Add all of the chicken to the skillet. Simmer, covered, for 10 minutes or until tender and cooked through. Keep warm until serving time.

Approx Per Serving: Cal 328; Prot 48 g; Carbo 11 g; T Fat 9 g; 26% Calories from Fat; Chol 126 mg; Fiber 1 g; Sod 507 mg

MANDARIN ORANGE-PEAR SALAD

This refreshing salad, with its sweet-tart flavor, complements the menu. It is best when slightly chilled. If you haven't had time to take the cans out of the pantry, just chill them in the freezer for a few minutes while you prepare the rest of the menu. Just don't forget to take the cans out of the freezer!

4 lettuce leaves
1 (16-ounce) can pear halves, drained
1 (11-ounce) can mandarin oranges, drained
2 tablespoons light sour cream

METHOD:

1. Arrange the lettuce leaves on salad plates or crystal fruit dishes.
2. Place 2 pear halves and an equal number of orange slices on each plate. Top with a dollop of sour cream.

Approx Per Serving: Cal 124; Prot 1 g; Carbo 31 g; T Fat 1 g; 5% Calories from Fat; Chol 3 mg; Fiber 3 g; Sod 17 mg

Horseradish-Flavored Mashed Potatoes

Add a little zip to your usual mashed potatoes with a tiny bit of horseradish. You are in for a taste treat, and your family might not even guess that it's horseradish!

1 3/4 cups skim milk
1 1/2 cups instant potato flakes
2 tablespoons light sour cream
1/2 teaspoon prepared horseradish
1 teaspoon butter seasoning
1/2 teaspoon each salt and coarsely ground pepper

Microwave Method:

1. Pour the milk into a microwave-safe pitcher or bowl. Microwave on High (100%) for 2 to 3 minutes.
2. Add the potato flakes, beating until stiff. Stir in the sour cream, horseradish, butter seasoning, salt and pepper.
3. Microwave on Medium-High (70%) for 1 to 2 minutes longer or until heated through. Cover to keep warm until serving time.

Tip: *To reheat potatoes, microwave, covered, on High (100%) for 45 to 60 seconds. Stir and serve.*

Conventional Method:

1. Heat the milk in a 1 1/2-quart saucepan over medium heat. Add the potato flakes, stirring until stiff.
2. Add the sour cream, horseradish, butter seasoning, salt and pepper and mix well.

Approx Per Serving: Cal 96; Prot 5 g; Carbo 16 g; T Fat 1 g; 8% Calories from Fat; Chol 4 mg; Fiber <1 g; Sod 368 mg

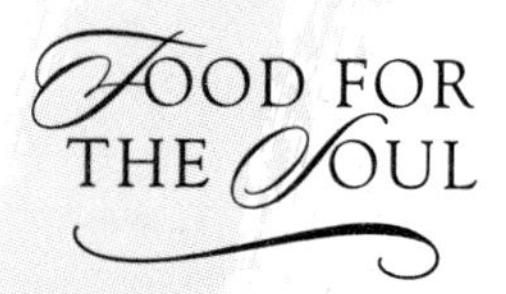

The secret is to act enthusiastic even though you may not feel enthusiastic and you will be amazed how enthusiasm takes over!

LET'S NOT ASSUME ANYTHING TODAY! WE CREATE MANY NEGATIVE SITUATIONS BY SIMPLY ASSUMING THAT OUR EXPECTATIONS ARE SELF-EVIDENT, AND THAT THEY ARE CLEARLY UNDERSTOOD AND SHARED BY OTHER PEOPLE.

—The 7 Habits of Highly Effective People

GREEN PEAS

Try adding 1 teaspoon butter seasoning to one 10-ounce package frozen green peas for a quick, simple way to get tasty, low-fat vegetables into your diet. Microwave using the package directions.

Approx Per Serving: Cal 51; Prot 3 g; Carbo 9 g; T Fat <1 g; 3% Calories from Fat; Chol <1 mg; Fiber 3 g; Sod 60 mg

POTATO ROLLS

Another way to keep those fat calories down is to butter your rolls lightly before serving and then keep them warm.

1 (8-count) package potato rolls
4 teaspoons reduced-fat margarine

METHOD:

1. Preheat the oven or toaster oven to 400 degrees.
2. Split potato rolls in half and spread with margarine.
3. Wrap potato rolls in foil and bake for approximately 4 to 6 minutes or until heated through.

Approx Per Serving: Cal 195; Prot 7 g; Carbo 26 g; T Fat 8 g; 35% Calories from Fat; Chol 0 mg; Fiber 2 g; Sod 285 mg

CHICKEN TERIYAKI

HERBED RICE

GREEN PEAS AND ONIONS

PINEAPPLE-CHERRY COTTAGE CHEESE SALAD

DINNER ROLLS

SERVES 4

DESSERT SUGGESTION:

Chocolate Cake (page 136)

WINE SUGGESTION:

Look for a fruity red wine for more depth of flavor. A white or red Zinfandel with good acidity will be a very good complement to this menu.

EN CONCERT:

Micro-cook the chicken while you prepare and cook the rice on the cooktop. Finish with micro-cooking the green peas and onions.

GROCERY LIST:

Groceries

- 4 skinless chicken breast fillets (2½ to 3 pounds)
- Fresh garlic *
- Fresh parsley
- 1 (4-ounce) package boil-in-bag rice *
- 1 (10-ounce) package frozen green peas and onions (without butter sauce)
- 1 (16-ounce) can sliced pineapple
- 1 (8-ounce) carton 1% cottage cheese
- 1 (4-ounce) jar maraschino cherries with stems
- 1 head iceberg lettuce
- Dinner rolls

Staples

- Teriyaki sauce
- Dried sweet basil
- Dried parsley
- Dried thyme
- Onion powder
- Reduced-fat margarine
- Salt and pepper
- Paprika
- Butter seasoning (i.e., Molly McButter)
- Nonstick vegetable cooking spray

*Note: Staples are items that are usually found in the pantry—look before ordering. An * denotes items that could be considered staples for some families.*

REFUSE TO ALLOW NEGATIVE THOUGHTS TO FORM COBWEBS IN YOUR MIND. BEFORE GOING TO SLEEP EACH NIGHT, GIVE YOURSELF A MENTAL "SHAMPOO," SUDSING OUT THE NEGATIVE AND VISUALIZING THE POSITIVE.

— Peale Center Plus Magazine

Chicken Teriyaki

This menu pairs the cooktop and the microwave with easy-to-prepare foods. You'll be eating in less than 30 minutes. Brushing the chicken breasts with this quick sauce creates a delicious Oriental tang, and the chicken is succulently moist.

4 skinless chicken breast fillets
2 cloves of garlic, crushed
1/4 cup teriyaki sauce
1 tablespoon freshly chopped parsley, or
  1 teaspoon dried parsley

En Concert Method:

1. Rinse the chicken and pat dry. Place in a 7x11-inch microwave-safe dish, with the thickest part of the chicken toward the outside edge. Cover with a lid or heavy plastic wrap, venting one corner.
2. Microwave on High (100%) for 8 to 10 minutes (3 1/2 minutes per pound) or until cooked through. Let stand, covered, for 5 minutes longer to finish cooking.
3. Spray a heavy skillet with nonstick vegetable cooking spray. Heat over medium-high heat. Add the chicken.
4. Brown on each side for 2 to 3 minutes; reduce the heat to medium.
5. Combine the garlic and teriyaki sauce in a small bowl. Brush over the chicken. Sprinkle with the parsley.
6. Cook, covered, for 8 to 10 minutes or until the juices run clear when pierced with a fork and the chicken is tender.

Approx Per Serving: Cal 160; Prot 28 g; Carbo 3 g; T Fat 3 g; 18% Calories from Fat; Chol 73 mg; Fiber <1 g; Sod 754 mg

Green Peas and Onions

One of the most popular of all vegetables can now be cooked right in the box, adding even more bright green eye appeal *and* more nutrition. Simply take one 10-ounce package frozen green peas and onions and remove any foil from the packaging. Place package on a paper plate and Microwave on High (100%) for 5 minutes, shaking gently. Serve immediately.

Approx Per Serving: Cal 53; Prot 3 g; Carbo 10 g; T Fat <1 g; 5% Calories from Fat; Chol 0 mg; Fiber 3 g; Sod 330 mg

HERBED RICE

1 (4-ounce) package boil-in-bag rice
1/2 teaspoon dried basil, or 1 tablespoon chopped fresh basil
1/2 teaspoon dried thyme
2 teaspoons onion powder
2 teaspoons butter seasoning
Salt and pepper to taste

METHOD:

1. Cook the rice using package directions. Spoon cooked rice into a saucepan.
2. Stir in the basil, thyme, onion powder, butter seasoning, salt and pepper. Simmer over low heat for 2 to 3 minutes longer. Cover and let stand until serving time.

Approx Per Serving: Cal 98; Prot 2 g; Carbo 22 g; T Fat <1 g; <1% Calories from Fat; Chol <1 mg; Fiber 0 g; Sod 10 mg

THOSE WHO WISH TO SING, ALWAYS FIND A SONG.

—Swedish Proverb

PINEAPPLE-CHERRY COTTAGE CHEESE

4 lettuce leaves, rinsed and dried
1 tablespoon paprika (optional)
1 (16-ounce) can sliced pineapple, drained
1 (8-ounce) carton 1% cottage cheese
4 maraschino cherries with stems

METHOD:

1. Dip the edges of each lettuce leaf in paprika. Place on individual salad plates.
2. Arrange 2 slices of pineapple over each lettuce leaf. Spoon cottage cheese into the center of each slice. Top with a cherry.

Approx Per Serving: Cal 113; Prot 8 g; Carbo 20 g; T Fat 1 g; 7% Calories from Fat; Chol 2 mg; Fiber 2 g; Sod 233 mg

DINNER ROLLS

Select bread with the best possible flavor from the bread counter, the bakery, or the freezer. This makes it easier not to use the "fat maker" butter. No matter what bread you choose, you are guiltless, as long as you do not use butter.

Sizzling Stir-Fry

STIR-FRY CHICKEN TERIYAKI SALAD

MINESTRONE

CRUSTY ITALIAN HERB BREAD

SERVES 4

DESSERT SUGGESTION:

Angel Short Cake (page 134)

WINE SUGGESTION:

Select a red or white Zinfandel with good acidity. A fruity red will add more depth of flavor. Either one will add pleasure!

EN CONCERT SEQUENCE:

Prepare everything ahead except for tossing the salad and dressing together. Your entrée is ready in a flash.

GROCERY LIST:

Groceries

1½ pounds skinless chicken breast fillets
1 (12-ounce) package mixed salad greens
1 red onion *
1 cucumber
1 bunch seedless green grapes
2 (10-ounce) cans minestrone
1 loaf Italian herb bread
Mint leaves or edible flowers

Staples

Brown sugar
Teriyaki sauce
Fresh garlic
Extra-virgin olive oil
Pecans
Strawberry Splash salad dressing
Balsamic vinegar
Confectioners' sugar
Nonstick vegetable cooking spray

*Note: Staples are items that are usually found in the pantry—look before ordering. An * denotes items that could be considered staples for some families.*

Stir-Fry Chicken Teriyaki Salad

Easy to prepare, yet filled with a delicious sweet-and-sour tang, this entrée is perfect for a picnic at home or a summer concert on the green. Prepare everything ahead, except for tossing the salad with the dressing. Your entrée is ready in a flash.

1 1/2 pounds skinless chicken breast fillets
1/2 cup teriyaki sauce
2 teaspoons brown sugar
2 large cloves of garlic, crushed
1 tablespoon extra-virgin olive oil
2 tablespoons pecans
1/2 cup Strawberry Splash salad dressing
2 teaspoons confectioners' sugar
1/4 cup balsamic vinegar
1/4 red onion, thinly sliced
1/2 cucumber, sliced
1/2 cup seedless green grapes, cut into halves
1 (12-ounce) package mixed salad greens, torn into bite-size pieces

En Concert Method:

1. Rinse the chicken and pat dry. Cut into 1/2x1-inch strips. Place in a shallow 2-quart dish.
2. Combine the teriyaki sauce, brown sugar, garlic and olive oil in a small bowl. Pour over the chicken. Marinate, covered, in the refrigerator for 30 to 60 minutes.
3. Spread the pecans in a glass plate. Microwave on High (100%) for 4 to 5 minutes or until golden brown; set aside.
4. Combine the salad dressing, confectioners' sugar and vinegar in a small jar. Cover and shake well to mix; set aside.
5. Drain the chicken, discarding the marinade.
6. Spray a large skillet with nonstick vegetable cooking spray. Preheat until very hot. Add half the chicken strips.
7. Stir-fry for 5 to 6 minutes or until cooked through. Remove from the skillet. Repeat the process with the remaining chicken.
8. Toss the onion, cucumber, grapes and salad greens in a salad bowl. Add the chicken, pecans and prepared dressing, tossing to coat. Serve immediately.

Approx Per Serving: Cal 415; Prot 39 g; Carbo 24 g; T Fat 18 g; 39% Calories from Fat; Chol 94 mg; Fiber 2 g; Sod 1721 mg

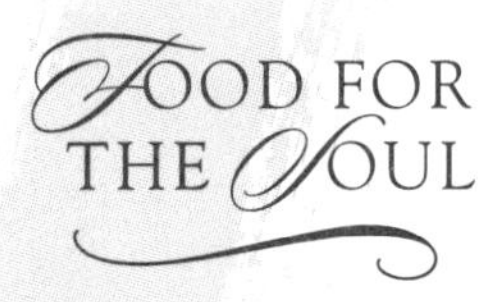

Love cures people—both the ones who give it and the ones who receive it.

—*Dr. Karl Menninger*

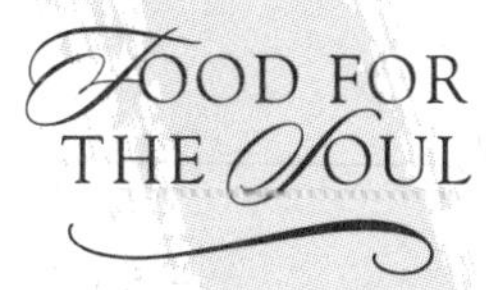

THE BEST AND MOST BEAUTIFUL THINGS IN THE WORLD CANNOT BE SEEN, NOR TOUCHED... BUT ARE FELT IN THE HEART.

—*Helen Keller*

MINESTRONE

There is something very satisfying about a bowl of hot soup. Select a light, broth-based minestrone from your shelf in the pantry to round out this menu. Voilà! It's ready when you are!

2 (10-ounce) cans ready-to-serve minestrone

METHOD:

1. Pour the soup into a microwave-safe bowl.
2. Microwave on High (100%) for 3 to 4 minutes or until heated through.

CRUSTY ITALIAN HERB BREAD

Find a good bakery department, and select a crusty herbed bread. I love the Italian bread I can get at my favorite supermarket bakery. Slice into thick slices and place on a foil-lined pan. To satisfy the need for butter, spread fat-free or light cream cheese on each slice, and sprinkle lightly with Parmesan cheese. Place in toaster oven or conventional oven and bake at 400 degrees for 3 to 4 minutes.

QUICK SKILLET SUPPER

TOSSED GREENS AND PEAR SALAD

TOAST POINTS

SERVES 6

DESSERT SUGGESTION:

Blueberry-Peach Crisp (page 140)

WINE SUGGESTION:

Select a Syrah or Rhône blend to enhance the sauce and mushrooms. It will also work well with the Peach-Blueberry Crisp.

EN CONCERT:

Prepare the skillet supper. While it is cooking, prepare the salad and toast points.

GROCERY LIST:

Groceries

1 pound round steak
1 envelope mushroom gravy mix
1 envelope spaghetti sauce mix
3 zucchini
1 green bell pepper
1 medium onion
2 packages boil-in-bag rice *
1 bunch fresh parsley
1 (12-ounce) package mixed salad greens
1 (4-ounce) package walnut pieces
1 Bosc pear

Staples

Vegetable oil and extra-virgin olive oil
Pepper
Nonstick vegetable cooking spray
Raspberry vinegar
Fresh garlic and garlic powder
Seasoned salt (i.e., Lawry's)
Sugar
Extra-light corn oil spread
Butter seasoning (i.e., Molly McButter)
1 loaf of bread

*Note: Staples are items that are usually found in the pantry—look before ordering. An * denotes items that could be considered staples for some families.*

FOOD FOR THE SOUL

THE SECRET OF ACHIEVEMENT IS NOT TO LET WHAT YOU ARE DOING GET TO YOU BEFORE YOU GET TO IT.

—Anonymous

Quick Skillet Supper

The term "comfort food" has been bandied about in the food industry for the past few years. It means recipes that bring back the happy memories of yesterday. This is a "comfort food" menu that is low in fat and takes a fraction of the time it took in years gone by, with the same great taste. A perfect blend of steak and veggies. Hooray for today's prepared foods and modern appliances! Happy memories.

1 teaspoon extra-virgin olive oil
1 pound round steak, cut into thin strips
1 envelope mushroom gravy mix
1 cup water
2 tablespoons spaghetti sauce mix
2 packages boil-in-bag rice
3 zucchini, cut into 1½-inch slices
1 green bell pepper, cut into thin strips
½ onion, thinly sliced
1 clove of garlic, crushed

En Concert Method:

1. Preheat a large skillet or electric skillet. Spray with nonstick vegetable cooking spray and add the olive oil. Add the round steak.
2. Cook until brown on all sides. Add the gravy mix, water and spaghetti sauce mix, stirring to mix well. Cook, covered, over low heat for 10 minutes, stirring occasionally.
3. Prepare the rice using package directions. Cover and keep warm.
4. Combine the zucchini, green pepper, onion and garlic in a 1½-quart microwave-safe dish.
5. Microwave, covered, on High (100%) for 4 to 5 minutes or until the vegetables are tender-crisp. Add to the steak mixture. Stir in the rice.
6. Simmer, covered, for 5 minutes longer. Remove from the heat and keep covered until serving time.

Approx Per Serving: Cal 278; Prot 22 g; Carbo 38 g; T Fat 4 g; 13% Calories from Fat; Chol 47 mg; Fiber 2 g; Sod 554 mg

Tossed Greens and Pear Salad

Ready in a flash and delicious. The fresh pear bites sprinkled in give a refreshing flavor, and the walnuts add more texture and taste.

2 tablespoons walnut pieces
1 Bosc pear
3 tablespoons raspberry vinegar
1/2 teaspoon sugar
1 teaspoon vegetable oil
1 (12-ounce) package mixed salad greens, chilled

Method:

1. Place the walnuts in a glass plate. Microwave on High (100%) for 3 to 4 minutes, stirring once from the outside to the center; set aside.
2. Peel, core and thinly slice the pear.
3. Combine the vinegar, sugar and oil in a glass jar; cover and shake to mix.
4. Place the salad greens, pear slices, walnuts and dressing in a large salad bowl, tossing to mix. Serve immediately.

Approx Per Serving: Cal 54; Prot 1 g; Carbo 7 g; T Fat 3 g; 39% Calories from Fat; Chol 0 mg; Fiber 2 g; Sod 15 mg

Toast Points

Have you ever been caught without any special rolls or bread in the house when something a little different seemed needed? Toast points add a little variety and are made from the usual bread around the kitchen. Tasty and guiltless!

For this easy and elegant recipe, first preheat the broiler. Then combine 1/4 teaspoon garlic powder, 1/4 teaspoon seasoned salt, 2 teaspoons extra-light corn oil spread and 2 teaspoons butter seasoning in a small dish. Spread the garlic powder mixture evenly over 6 toasted bread slices and place them on a foil-lined baking pan. Broil 6 inches from the heat source until golden brown. Slice each piece of toast into 4 triangles. Serve immediately.

Approx Per Serving: Cal 104; Prot 3 g; Carbo 17 g; T Fat 3 g; 22% Calories from Fat; Chol 1 mg; Fiber 1 g; Sod 225 mg

Make no little plans; they have no magic to stir men's blood and probably themselves will not be realized. Make big plans; aim high in hope and work, remembering that a noble, logical diagram, once recorded, will not die.

—Daniel Burnham

HEAVENLY HAM

PARSLIED NEW POTATOES

GREEN BEANS WITH ONIONS AND PIMENTOS

ONION ROLLS

SERVES 6

DESSERT SUGGESTION:

Sweet Ambrosia (page 151)

WINE SUGGESTION:

A good Beaujolais, Côtes du Rhône, Pinot Noir, or white Zinfandel are excellent choices. A Chenin Blanc will give a slightly more off-dry wine flavor and will also be good.

EN CONCERT:

Begin with the ham. While it is cooking, prepare the new potatoes and green beans.

GROCERY LIST:

Groceries

1 (3 1/2-pound) fully-cooked, 97% fat-free ham
1 orange
1 bunch fresh parsley
1 pint bourbon or rum *
12 small red potatoes
2 (10-ounce) packages frozen French-style green beans *
or 2 (16-ounce) cans French-style green beans
1 (4-ounce) jar sliced pimentos
12 prepared onion rolls

Staples

Brown sugar
Flour
Dry mustard
Fat-free butter seasoning (i.e., Molly McButter)
Reduced-fat butter
Fat-free margarine
Salt and pepper
Nonstick vegetable cooking spray

*Note: Staples are items that are usually found in the pantry—look before ordering. An * denotes items that could be considered staples for some families.*

Heavenly Ham

Ham and spring dinners just go hand in hand. Yet, ham has always been synonymous with thoughts of high fat content and long cooking. Hooray, for today, and low-fat and fat-free ham which has arrived and fits in easily with our hectic schedules. This delicious Bourbon Glaze (don't worry, the alcohol is cooked off) is ready in a jiffy and creates a divine flavor. Save the leftovers for great sandwiches.

1 (3½-pound) 97% fat-free, ready-to-eat ham, thinly sliced
Bourbon Glaze
1 orange, thinly sliced
1 bunch fresh parsley

Microwave Method:

1. Place the ham slices in a 2-quart microwave-safe dish. Spread with the Bourbon Glaze.
2. Microwave on Medium (70%) for 3 to 4 minutes or until heated through. Keep covered until ready to serve. Garnish with orange slices and parsley.

Conventional Method:

1. Place the ham slices in a 10-inch skillet sprayed with nonstick cooking spray. Pour the hot Bourbon Glaze evenly over the ham.
2. Simmer until heated through. Cover to keep warm.

Approx Per Serving: Cal 230; Prot 33 g; Carbo 11 g; T Fat 5 g; 19% Calories from Fat; Chol 88 mg; Fiber 1 g; Sod 495 mg
Nutritional information based on nine servings.

Bourbon Glaze

The trick is to not use too much. Let the meat marinate for 20 minutes to achieve the best flavor. Use any leftover glaze to marinate chicken or pork. Rum is equally good in this sauce.

To prepare the sauce combine ½ cup packed brown sugar, 1½ tablespoons flour and ½ teaspoon dry mustard in a 2-cup glass measure. Mix until throughly combined. Stir in 2 tablespoons bourbon. Then microwave on High (100%) for 45 to 60 seconds; stir well.

For a Conventional Method combine the brown sugar, flour, mustard and bourbon in a 1-quart saucepan and cook over medium-high heat until hot and bubbly, stirring constantly.

No pessimist ever discovered the secrets of the stars, or sailed to an uncharted land, or opened a new heaven to the human spirit.

—Helen Keller

FOOD FOR THE SOUL

ADVICE IS LIKE SNOW; THE SOFTER IT FALLS, THE LONGER IT DWELLS UPON, AND THE DEEPER IT SINKS INTO, THE MIND.

—Samuel Taylor Coleridge

PARSLIED NEW POTATOES

Your microwave oven is the ideal means for cooking these new potatoes. You will achieve an especially delicious flavor and get more nutrition to boot! Remember, only 2 tablespoons of water to 1 quart of fresh vegetables. The new fat-free butter seasoning is a great partner for cutting down on the fat while retaining the traditional taste.

12 small new potatoes, cut into halves
1 tablespoon water
1 tablespoon fat-free butter seasoning
1 teaspoon reduced-fat butter
2 tablespoons chopped fresh parsley
Pepper and salt to taste

MICROWAVE METHOD:

1. Arrange the potatoes in a 2-quart microwave-safe dish. Add the water, butter seasoning, butter, parsley and pepper; cover with a lid or plastic wrap with a small vent.
2. Microwave on High (100%) for 6 to 8 minutes or until fork-tender. Sprinkle with salt and serve.

CONVENTIONAL METHOD:

1. Combine the potatoes, butter seasoning, butter, parsley, pepper, salt and 1 cup water in a 2-quart saucepan. Cover tightly.
2. Bring to a boil; reduce the heat. Simmer for 20 to 25 minutes or until the potatoes are fork-tender. Drain well and serve.

Approx Per Serving: Cal 208; Prot 4 g; Carbo 47 g; T Fat 1 g; 2% Calories from Fat; Chol 1 mg; Fiber 4 g; Sod 29 mg

Green Beans with Onions and Pimentos

Always a favorite, green beans are very adaptable. They make great partners with a variety of other vegetables and condiments, such as this trio—bright, tasty, AND nutritious. Choose frozen or canned green beans for speedy preparation.

2 (10-ounce) packages frozen French-style green beans, or
  2 (16-ounce) cans French-style green beans
1 (8-ounce) jar pearl onions, drained
2 tablespoons sliced pimentos
1 tablespoon fat-free margarine or butter seasoning
Salt and pepper to taste

Microwave Method:

1. Place the beans in a 2-quart microwave-safe dish, breaking up the beans with a fork. (If using canned beans, drain off the liquid.)
2. Add the onions, pimentos, margarine, salt and pepper. Microwave, covered, on High (100%) for 3½ to 6 minutes or until tender-crisp. Serve immediately.

Conventional Method:

1. Place the beans in a 2-quart saucepan. Add the onions, pimentos, margarine, salt and pepper.
2. Cook, covered, using package directions and stirring occasionally. (If using canned beans, do not drain.)

Approx Per Serving: Cal 33; Prot 2 g; Carbo 7 g; T Fat <1 g; 5% Calories from Fat; Chol 0 mg; Fiber 3 g; Sod 18 mg

Onion Rolls

A good way to forget about butter is to take advantage of the many tasty specialty breads or rolls now available in our bakeries and stores. Onion rolls complement this menu with their pungent flavor and crunchy texture. Simply place 12 onion rolls on a foil-lined pan. Place in a preheated 425-degree oven. Heat the rolls for 5 to 8 minutes or until warm and crispy. Serve immediately or wrap in foil and keep warm until serving time.

Nutritional information for this recipe is not available.

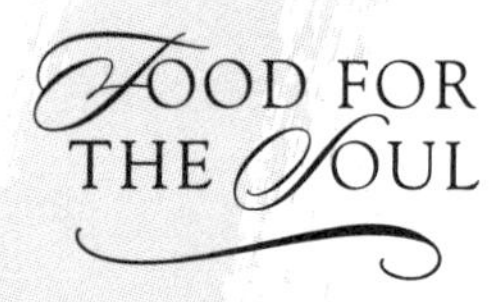

All accomplishments, actions and fears are stimulated first by dreams. They keep people...alive. Keep your dreams and keep hope going—always!

—Peale Center for Christian Living

TONY'S PASTA MAGNIFICO

TOSSED GREEN SALAD WITH TOASTED WALNUTS AND MARINATED ARTICHOKES

ITALIAN BREAD

SERVES 4

DESSERT SUGGESTION:

Low-fat vanilla frozen yogurt with "M & M's" Chocolate Candies

WINE SUGGESTION:

A Chianti complements this menu and adds both color and ambiance for delightful conviviality.

EN CONCERT:

Cook the pasta on the cooktop while you cut up the vegetables and cook them in the skillet. Toast the walnuts in the microwave and toss salad together just before serving.

GROCERY LIST:

Groceries

1 (16-ounce) package penne pasta
3 plum tomatoes
1 red bell pepper
1 yellow bell pepper
2 medium purple onions
1 head fresh garlic *
1 bunch fresh parsley
5 ounces Parmesan cheese
1 (4-ounce) package walnut pieces
1 (6-ounce) jar marinated artichoke hearts
1 head romaine *
1 (6-ounce) package garlic croutons *
1 loaf Italian bread

Staples

Lemon juice
Extra-virgin olive oil
Pepper
Nonstick vegetable cooking spray
Balsamic vinegar
Confectioners' sugar

*Note: Staples are items that are usually found in the pantry—look before ordering. An * denotes items that could be considered staples for some families.*

Tony's Pasta Magnifico

Growing up in a little village in Italy, my friend Tony has many fond memories of gratifying pasta dishes. This is a favorite. It is prepared in a flash, yet the delicious flavor and beautiful color make it look complicated. It's the perfect new-age recipe with old-country flavor and appeal. Buon appetito!

3 plum tomatoes
1 (16-ounce) package penne
1 red bell pepper
1 yellow bell pepper
1 medium purple onion
1 teaspoon extra-virgin olive oil
4 medium cloves of garlic, crushed
1 teaspoon lemon juice
Freshly ground pepper to taste
1/2 cup freshly grated Parmesan cheese
1/4 cup freshly chopped parsley

Method:

1. Bring 3 quarts of water to a boil in a large stockpot. Drop in the tomatoes and blanche for 30 seconds. Remove with a slotted spoon. Peel and discard the skin; let stand to cool slightly.
2. Add the pasta to the boiling water. Cook until al dente (just tender).
3. Chop the tomatoes, bell peppers and onion while the pasta cooks.
4. Preheat a heavy skillet sprayed with nonstick cooking spray over high heat. Add the olive oil; reduce the heat to medium. Add the garlic, onion, bell peppers, lemon juice and pepper, stirring well. Add the tomatoes.
5. Simmer for 5 to 6 minutes.
6. Drain the pasta and place on a serving platter or on individual serving plates. Spoon the vegetable mixture over the pasta; top with Parmesan cheese and parsley. Serve immediately.

Approx Per Serving: Cal 530; Prot 21 g; Carbo 95 g; T Fat 7 g; 12% Calories from Fat; Chol 10 mg; Fiber 5 g; Sod 249 mg

Tip: *Be sure the pasta is hot before serving. Heat individual servings in the microwave on Medium-High (80%) for 30 to 45 seconds each, or if using a platter, microwave for 2 to 3 minutes.*

A happy person is not a person with a certain set of circumstances, but rather a person with a certain set of attitudes.

—*Hugh Downs*

POSITIVE ATTITUDES DRAW POSITIVE RESULTS!

—*Norman Vincent Peale*

TOSSED GREEN SALAD WITH TOASTED WALNUTS AND MARINATED ARTICHOKES

Crispy fresh greens and crunchy toasted walnuts give this salad the texture to complement the softer pasta, adding interest with optimum flavor.

2 tablespoons walnut pieces
5 marinated artichoke hearts, cut into halves
1 head romaine, torn into bite-size pieces
1/4 purple onion, thinly sliced
1/2 cup prepared garlic croutons
1/4 cup balsamic vinegar
1 teaspoon confectioners' sugar
2 tablespoons artichoke liquid

METHOD:

1. Spread the walnuts in a glass dish. Microwave on High (100%) for 3 to 5 minutes or until toasted, stirring once from the outside edge to the middle.
2. Combine the artichokes with the romaine, walnuts, onion and croutons in a salad bowl.
3. Whisk the vinegar, confectioners' sugar and artichoke liquid in a small bowl. Pour over the salad, tossing to coat. Serve immediately.

Approx Per Serving: Cal 117; Prot 3 g; Carbo 13 g; T Fat 7 g; 48% Calories from Fat; Chol <1 mg; Fiber 3 g; Sod 296 mg
Nutritional information does not include the artichoke marinade.

ITALIAN BREAD

Buy the freshest bread you can find and don't use butter. If you feel you have to have a little more flavor, mix 3 tablespoons of olive oil and 1 small clove of crushed garlic in a saucer and spread lightly over the bread.

Nutritional information for this recipe is not available.

SPEEDY PIZZA

BUTTER LETTUCE SALAD WITH RASPBERRY-POPPY SEED VINAIGRETTE

SERVES 4

DESSERT SUGGESTION:

Low-fat vanilla or chocolate creme cookies

WINE SUGGESTION:

Merlot or Light Chianti

EN CONCERT:

Set the oven temperature. Cook the vegetables while you are pouring the sauce over the pizza dough. Toss the salad while the pizza is baking.

GROCERY LIST:

Groceries

1 (16-ounce) prepared pizza shell (i.e., Boboli)
1 (8-ounce) package marinara sauce
1 (8-ounce) package shredded low-fat mozzarella cheese
1 medium green bell pepper *
1 medium red bell pepper *
1 medium yellow bell pepper *
1 medium zucchini
1 bunch broccoli
1 large head butter lettuce
1 (6-ounce) jar marinated artichoke hearts
1 (4-ounce) package dried tart cherries or dried apricots

Staples:

Raspberry vinaigrette
Poppy seeds
Fresh garlic
1 onion
Nonstick cooking spray
Walnut pieces

*Note: Staples are items that are usually found in the pantry—look before ordering. An * denotes items that could be considered staples for some families.*

FOOD FOR THE SOUL

CHERISH YOUR VISIONS AND YOUR DREAMS AS THEY ARE THE CHILDREN OF YOUR SOUL; THE BLUEPRINTS OF YOUR ULTIMATE ACHIEVEMENTS.

—Napoleon Hill

SPEEDY PIZZA

Try this "scratch quick" menu when you are hungry but just aren't in the mood for spending time in the kitchen. All of the ingredients can be picked up at your convenience and stay in your refrigerator and pantry for a week. Pizza is an all-American favorite. Just pour on the ingredients, and voilà! It's ready to eat in less than 15 minutes!

1 (16-ounce) prepared pizza shell (i.e., Boboli)
1 (8-ounce) package marinara sauce
1 large clove of garlic, crushed
1/3 cup chopped onion
1/3 cup chopped red bell pepper
1/3 cup chopped green bell pepper
1/3 cup chopped yellow bell pepper
1/3 cup chopped zucchini
1/3 cup chopped broccoli
1 (8-ounce) package shredded low-fat mozzarella cheese

METHOD:

1. Place the pizza shell on a 12-inch pizza pan. Pour the marinara sauce evenly over the shell.
2. Spray a skillet with nonstick cooking spray. Heat over medium heat. Add the garlic, onion, bell peppers, zucchini and broccoli.
3. Sauté for 2 to 3 minutes or until tender-crisp. Sprinkle evenly over the pizza. Top with the cheese.
4. Bake in preheated 425-degree oven for 10 to 12 minutes. Serve immediately.

Approx Per Serving: Cal 611; Prot 30 g; Carbo 91 g; T Fat 17 g; 24% Calories from Fat; Chol 31 mg; Fiber 4 g; Sod 1497 mg

Butter Lettuce Salad with Raspberry-Poppy Seed Vinaigrette

This is a great way to get in at least one of the five-per-day servings of fruit and vegetables found to be so important to reduce the risk of cancer. This salad's slightly buttery taste is especially appealing when paired with the zip and texture of the pizza.

3 tablespoons walnuts, toasted
1 large head butter lettuce, torn into bite-size pieces
4 marinated artichoke hearts, cut into halves
2 tablespoons artichoke liquid
2 tablespoons dried tart cherries or dried apricots, cut up
1/4 cup raspberry vinaigrette
1/2 teaspoon poppy seeds

Method:

1. Place walnuts in a glass pie plate. Microwave on High (100%) for 3 to 6 minutes or until lightly toasted.
2. Combine the lettuce, artichokes, artichoke liquid, walnuts and cherries in a salad bowl.
3. Mix the vinaigrette with the poppy seeds in a covered jar. Pour over the salad.
4. Toss gently to coat before serving.

Approx Per Serving: Cal 158; Prot 3 g; Carbo 10 g; T Fat 14 g; 70% Calories from Fat; Chol <1 mg; Fiber 3 g; Sod 299 mg
Nutritional information does not include the artichoke marinade.

There is an ebb and flow in the tide of human life. When everything goes against you, and it seems you cannot hold a minute longer, never give up. The tide will turn.

—Peale Center for Christian Living

THE MAGNIFICENT POTATO

TOSSED GREEN SALAD WITH LIGHT CAESAR DRESSING

FRENCH OR ITALIAN BREAD

SERVES 4

DESSERT SUGGESTION:

Cinnamon Baked Apples (page 139)

EN CONCERT:

The key to this menu is the *en concert* technique. Bake the potato and let it stand, wrapped in a paper towel, or pop into the toaster oven and bake at 400 degrees for 5 minutes to really crisp the skin while you prepare the sauce; cover. Cook the bacon (it needs to stand a bit to become crisp) and last cook the broccoli.

GROCERY LIST:

Groceries:

4 large baking potatoes *
1 bunch broccoli
1 (16-ounce) package bacon *
8 ounces shredded low-fat sharp Cheddar cheese *
1 (16-ounce) package mixed salad greens *
1 loaf French or Italian bread

Staples

Salt and pepper
Light mayonnaise
Skim milk
Light Caesar salad dressing

*Note: Staples are items that are usually found in the pantry—look before ordering. An * denotes items that could be considered staples for some families.*

The Magnificent Potato

The stuffed potato really becomes magnificent when you can come home, change into your sweats, and feed the group in less than 30 minutes, start to finish. This is the "fast lane" supper. Pile on these easy fixin's and enjoy.

4 large baking potatoes
1 bunch broccoli, broken up into florets, chopped
3 slices lean bacon
1/2 cup light mayonnaise
1/2 cup skim milk
3/4 to 1 cup shredded low-fat sharp Cheddar cheese

En Concert Method:

1. Preheat the oven or toaster oven to 400 degrees. Rinse and dry the potatoes; pierce several times with a fork. Arrange on microwave-safe rack in microwave. Microwave on High (100%) for 15 minutes, turning once.
2. Rinse the broccoli and wrap in a nonrecycled white paper towel. Sprinkle with water and place seam side down on a paper plate. Place the bacon between 2 paper towels on a paper plate.
3. Mix the mayonnaise, milk and cheese in a 2-cup glass measure. Remove the potatoes from the microwave and place in preheated oven. Bake for 5 to 6 minutes while preparing the toppings.
4. Microwave cheese mixture on High (100%) for 3 to 4 minutes, stirring twice. Remove, stir and set aside. Microwave broccoli on High (100%) for 3 to 3 1/2 minutes or until tender-crisp. Let stand, covered, for 2 to 3 minutes. Microwave bacon on High (100%) for 2 to 3 minutes or until crispy; crumble.
5. Remove potatoes from oven and place on individual serving plates. Roll gently and open with a fork. Top with the broccoli, cheese sauce and crumbled bacon. Serve immediately.

Approx Per Serving: Cal 432; Prot 15 g; Carbo 55 g; T Fat 18 g; 36% Calories from Fat; Chol 41 mg; Fiber 5 g; Sod 440 mg

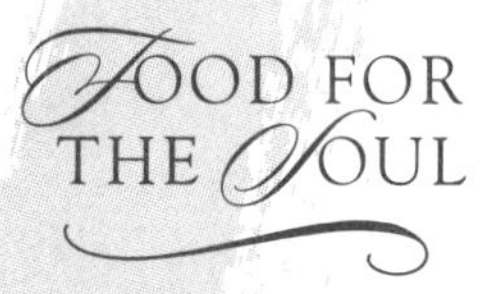

The only place that success comes before work is in the dictionary.

—Donald Kendall

Tossed Green Salad and Bread

To round out the menu, toss one 16-ounce package mixed salad greens with 1 cup light Caesar salad dressing and serve with a loaf of crusty French or Italian bread.

45 MINUTES OR LESS

Menus

THERE ARE MANY WAYS TO GIVE THE SAME RECIPE A NEW AND SOMETIMES DIFFERENT LOOK.

HERE ARE A FEW IDEAS FOR WAYS TO CHANGE THE FLAVOR AND CREATE A NEW TASTE TREAT.

VEGETABLES

Mashed Potatoes
- * 1 to 2 tablespoons mint jelly to the milk, especially when serving lamb
- * 1/4 teaspoon lemon pepper

New Potatoes
- * 1 teaspoon reduced-fat butter and 1 cup frozen peas
- * 1 teaspoon reduced-fat butter and 1/2 cup chopped onion

Green Beans
- * 1 (8-ounce) can Mexican- or Italian-seasoned tomatoes, drained
- * 1/2 cup medium salsa
- * 3 pieces bacon, crisp-cooked in microwave, crumbled
- * 3 tablespoons toasted walnuts or pecans

Green Peas
- * 2 tablespoons chopped roasted red peppers
- * 1 (6-ounce) can pearl onions, drained

Carrots
- * 3 to 4 tablespoons raisins and 1 teaspoon brown sugar
- * 1 tablespoon brown sugar and 1/2 cup mini marshmallows
- * 1 teaspoon each Vermouth, reduced-fat butter and confectioners' sugar

Corn
- * 1 (16-ounce) can lima beans, drained, and 1 teaspoon reduced-fat butter

* *indicates each flavor suggestion*

FISH

Sole, swordfish, orange roughy, whitefish or scrod
- * Spread the top with any of the following: honey mustard; commercial chutney; or balsamic vinegar and garlic sauce before cooking.
- * Or, try rolling in walnuts, pecans or chestnuts which have been crushed and toasted in the microwave.

Salmon
- * Hollandaise sauce
- * Tomato chutney (page 110)
- * Dash of lemon pepper

MEAT

Pork
- * 1/2 sliced apple per serving and cinnamon candies. Wrap apples and candies in heavy plastic wrap and microwave on High for 1 to 2 minutes.
- * Spread with mild pepper relish.
- * Spread with cranberry mustard sauce. (page 18)

Ham
- * Spread with cranberry mustard sauce.
- * Top with mixture of 2 teaspoons brown sugar and 1/2 cup pineapple juice or crushed pineapple. Heat through.

Chicken
- * Marinate in Italian salad dressing for 15 to 30 minutes.

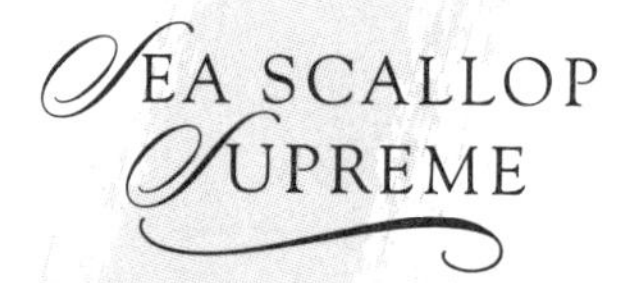

BREADED SEA SCALLOPS

BAKED POTATOES AND CHEESE

HEAVENLY BABY CARROTS

SLICED TOMATOES VINAIGRETTE

FRENCH BREAD OR ROLLS

SERVES 4

Dessert Suggestion:

Strawberry-Tapioca Swirl (page 150)

Wine Suggestion:

Chardonnay from the Carneros, central coast of California, or the finer lakes of New York. Look for a Chardonnay that is dry with good acidity.

En Concert Sequence:

Micro-cook the potatoes first, then prepare the tomatoes and marinate them while the carrots are cooking and lastly the scallops. Keep food covered after cooking.

Grocery List:

Groceries

- 1 pound fresh sea scallops
- 4 medium (5-ounce) baking potatoes
- 1 cup shredded fat-free Cheddar cheese
- 1 bunch chives or green onions
- 1 package fresh or frozen baby carrots
- 4 medium tomatoes
- 1 loaf French bread or French rolls
- Fresh parsley
- Vermouth

Staples

- Seasoned bread crumbs
- Garlic powder, paprika, dried parsley, black pepper
- Raisins
- Confectioners' sugar
- Fat-free French salad dressing
- Reduced-fat margarine
- Nonstick vegetable cooking spray
- Salt

Note: Staples are items that are usually found in the pantry—look before ordering.

TAKE A STEP AT A TIME TOWARD YOUR GOAL. THE JOURNEY OF A THOUSAND MILES BEGINS WITH ONE STEP.

—Lao-Tse

BREADED SEA SCALLOPS

Succulently moist with a slightly crisp delicious flavor. Ready in a flash!

1/2 cup seasoned bread crumbs
1/2 teaspoon garlic powder
1/2 teaspoon paprika
1 tablespoon chopped fresh parsley, or 1 teaspoon dried parsley
1 pound fresh sea scallops

MICROWAVE METHOD:

1. Combine the seasoned bread crumbs, garlic powder, paprika and parsley in a sealable plastic bag. Seal the bag and shake to mix well.
2. Rinse the scallops and pat dry with a paper towel. Add to the seasonings and shake to coat evenly.
3. Arrange the scallops in a 1 1/2-quart microwave-safe dish. Cover with heavy plastic wrap venting one corner, or cover with a lid.
4. Microwave on High (100%) for 3 to 4 minutes or until the scallops pierce easily with a fork and are nearly opaque. Stir gently. Let stand, covered, for 5 minutes to finish cooking.

CONVENTIONAL METHOD:

1. Preheat the oven to 400 degrees.
2. Follow Microwave Method Steps 1 and 2.
3. Place the coated scallops on a baking sheet sprayed with nonstick vegetable cooking spray.
4. Bake for 10 to 15 minutes or until the scallops pierce easily with a fork and are opaque. Cover with foil until ready to serve.

Approx Per Serving: Cal 116; Prot 11 g; Carbo 12 g; T Fat 2 g; 17% Calories from Fat; Chol 18 mg; Fiber 1 g; Sod 631 mg

Baked Potatoes and Cheese

We call them Irish, but potatoes originated in Peru, where they were first cured by frost and then dried. Now we can have them fluffy and delicious in mere minutes with the magic of the microwave oven!

4 medium (5-ounce) baking potatoes
1 cup shredded fat-free Cheddar cheese
1/4 cup finely chopped chives or green onions

Microwave Method:

1. Rinse the potatoes well and pierce all the way through.
2. Place in the microwave oven (preferably on a rack) with space between each potato. Microwave on High (100%) for 14 to 16 minutes or until slightly firm to the touch but not hard.
3. Mix the cheese and chopped chives in a small bowl while the potatoes cook.
4. Wrap the potatoes in a paper towel to keep them more crisp, and let stand for up to 20 minutes. Open with a fork and top with the cheese mixture.

En Concert Method (Microwave and Conventional):

1. Preheat the oven to 450 degrees.
2. Follow Microwave Method Steps 1 and 2 except microwave the potatoes on High (100%) for 12 to 14 minutes.
3. Bake in preheated conventional oven for 5 to 10 minutes or until the skins are crisp. Follow Microwave Method Steps 3 and 4.

Conventional Method:

1. Preheat the oven to 425 degrees.
2. Follow Microwave Method Step 3.
3. Rinse the potatoes and rub with nonstick cooking spray.
4. Place the potatoes on the middle oven rack and bake for 35 to 45 minutes or until tender. Let stand for several minutes before serving. Open and top with the cheese mixture.

Approx Per Serving: Cal 149; Prot 8 g; Carbo 30 g; T Fat <1 g; 1% Calories from Fat; Chol 2 mg; Fiber 3 g; Sod 119 mg

When we truly care for ourselves, it becomes possible to care far more profoundly about other people. The more alert and sensitive we are to our own needs, the more loving and generous we can be toward others.

—Eda LeShan

Start preparing for happy old age when you are young. If you are tight with money at thirty, you will be a miser at seventy.

Heavenly Baby Carrots

1 teaspoon confectioners' sugar
1/4 teaspoon dry vermouth
2 teaspoons reduced-fat margarine
2 tablespoons raisins
1 (10-ounce) package fresh or frozen baby carrots
Salt to taste

Microwave Method:

1. Combine the confectioners' sugar, wine, margarine and raisins with 2 tablespoons water in a 1-quart microwave-safe dish and mix well. Add the carrots.
2. Cover and microwave on High (100%) for 5 to 6 minutes, stirring once. Season with salt to taste. Serve immediately.

Conventional Method:

1. Bring 1 inch of water to a boil in a 1 1/2-quart saucepan. Add salt and carrots. Cook for 15 minutes or until fork tender; drain.
2. Add the confectioners' sugar, wine, margarine and raisins and mix gently. Simmer for 1 to 2 minutes longer.

Approx Per Serving: Cal 58; Prot 1 g; Carbo 12 g; T Fat 1 g; 19% Calories from Fat; Chol 0 mg; Fiber 2 g; Sod 55 mg

Sliced Tomatoes Vinaigrette

Once known as love apples and considered poisonous, tomatoes are now one of our best-liked vegetables and healthy, too! For this quick and easy salad slice 4 medium tomatoes and arrange them on a serving plate. Drizzle 1/4 cup fat-free French salad dressing over the top and then sprinkle with black pepper to taste. Garnish with fresh parsley.

Approx Per Serving: Cal 46; Prot 1 g; Carbo 12 g; T Fat <1 g; 7% Calories from Fat; Chol 0 mg; Fiber 2 g; Sod 161 mg

French Bread

Choose your favorite crunchy bread and enjoy!

1/2 cup fat-free cream cheese, softened
2 green onions, finely chopped
1 clove of garlic, crushed
6 slices French bread

Method:

1. Preheat the broiler.
2. Combine the cream cheese, green onions and garlic in a bowl and mix well.
3. Spread the mixture over the bread slices. Arrange on a baking sheet. Broil for 4 minutes or just until bubbly. Serve immediately.

Approx Per Serving: Cal 89; Prot 5 g; Carbo 15 g; T Fat 1 g; 10% Calories from Fat; Chol 2 mg; Fiber 1 g; Sod 259 mg

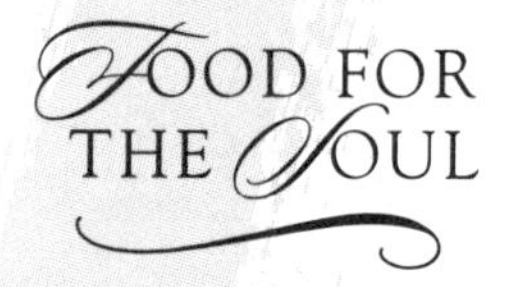

If you talk a lot at thirty, you will be a windbag at seventy. If you are kind and thoughtful at thirty, you will be lovable at seventy.

—Anonymous

VERACRUZ-STYLE SNAPPER

PARSLEY AND HERBED RICE

CHEESY ZUCCHINI

TOSSED GREEN SALAD WITH MANDARIN ORANGES

SERVES 4

DESSERT SUGGESTION:

Low-fat mint chocolate chip ice cream

WINE SUGGESTION:

A vibrantly fruity Sauvignon Blanc with a sassy herbal edge and little or no oak. It will then not overwhelm the subtleties of the fish, yet will balance the spice of the Veracruz flavor.

EN CONCERT:

Cook rice on the stovetop. While the rice is cooking, micro-cook the snapper, and then the cheesy zucchini.

GROCERY LIST:

Groceries

- 1 (2½-pound) red snapper fillet
- 1 medium yellow onion
- 1 (29-ounce) can solid-pack tomatoes
- 1 (7-ounce) jar stuffed green olives
- 1 small jar capers
- 4 medium zucchini
- 8 ounces fat-free sharp Cheddar cheese
- 1 package long grain white rice
- 2 chicken bouillon cubes
- 1 head red lettuce
- 1 head Bibb lettuce
- 1 (8-ounce) can mandarin oranges
- 1 medium purple onion *

Staples

- Olive oil
- Salt and pepper
- Nonstick vegetable cooking spray
- Dried parsley, tarragon, thyme and oregano
- Dry mustard
- Poppy seeds
- Butter substitute
- Dried chopped onion
- Raspberry vinegar
- Confectioners' sugar

*Note: Staples are items that are usually found in the pantry—look before ordering. An * denotes items that could be considered staples for some families.*

Veracruz-Style Snapper

If you ever thought that all fish tastes the same—bland—try this truly tasty red snapper recipe. Fish is naturally low in fat, good for you, and very versatile. Paired with a menu filled with a variety of complementary dishes, it's a winner! Enjoy!

1 teaspoon olive oil
1 medium yellow onion, chopped
1 (29-ounce) can solid-pack tomatoes
1/2 (7-ounce) jar stuffed green olives, cut into halves
1 tablespoon capers
Salt and pepper to taste
1 (2 1/2-pound) red snapper fillet

Microwave Method:

1. Spray a 1-quart microwave-safe dish with nonstick vegetable cooking spray and add the olive oil and onion. Microwave on High (100%) for 2 to 3 minutes.
2. Add the tomatoes, olives, capers, salt and pepper. Microwave on High (100%) for 2 minutes longer.
3. Place the snapper in a shallow 2-quart microwave-safe dish with a lid. Pour 1/3 of the tomato mixture over the top. Cover and microwave on High (100%) for 3 minutes.
4. Add the remaining tomato mixture. Microwave for 4 to 6 minutes longer or until the fish flakes easily with a fork. Let stand, covered, for 5 minutes before serving.

Conventional Method:

1. Spray a 1-quart saucepan generously with nonstick vegetable cooking spray and add the olive oil and onion. Sauté over low heat until the onion is tender.
2. Add the tomatoes, olives, capers, salt and pepper. Cook, covered, over medium heat for 5 minutes, stirring occasionally.
3. Spray a 10-inch skillet with nonstick vegetable cooking spray and heat. Add the fish and the tomato mixture. Cook, covered, for 20 minutes or until the fish flakes easily with a fork.

Approx Per Serving: Cal 279; Prot 42 g; Carbo 12 g; T Fat 7 g; 23% Calories from Fat; Chol 70 mg; Fiber 3 g; Sod 1064 mg

Let your mind be quiet, realizing the beauty of the world, and the immense, the boundless treasure that it holds in store.

—*Edward Carpenter*

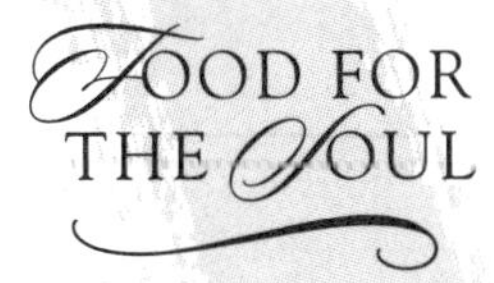

PUTTERING IS REALLY A TIME TO BE ALONE, TO DREAM AND TO GET IN TOUCH WITH YOURSELF... TO PUTTER IS TO DISCOVER.

—*Alexandra Stoddard*

CHEESY ZUCCHINI

Zucchini, one of the most versatile of the squash family, is delicious and nutritious paired with fat-free sharp Cheddar cheese. Add a little pepper for punch.

4 medium zucchini
1 teaspoon butter substitute
Pepper to taste
3 slices fat-free sharp Cheddar cheese
Salt to taste

MICROWAVE METHOD:

1. Rinse the squash and cut into 1/2-inch pieces, discarding the ends. Combine with the butter substitute, pepper and 2 tablespoons water in a 1 1/2-quart microwave-safe dish with a lid.
2. Microwave, covered, on High (100%) for 4 to 6 minutes; stir gently. Arrange the cheese over the top. Microwave, covered, for 30 seconds longer.
3. Let stand, covered, until serving time. Season with salt to taste. Microwave on Medium-High (70%) for 45 to 90 seconds to reheat if necessary.

CONVENTIONAL METHOD:

1. Rinse the squash and cut into 1/2-inch pieces, discarding the ends. Add the cut squash to 1 inch of boiling water in a 1 1/2-quart saucepan. Add the butter substitute, salt and pepper.
2. Bring to a rolling boil and reduce the heat. Simmer for 6 to 8 minutes or until fork tender; drain.
3. Arrange the cheese over the top. Let stand, covered, for 1 minute or until the cheese melts. Serve immediately.

Approx Per Serving: Cal 40; Prot 4 g; Carbo 7 g; T Fat <1 g; 5% Calories from Fat; Chol <1 mg; Fiber 2 g; Sod 127 mg

Parsley and Herbed Rice

1 cup long grain white rice
2 cups hot water
2 chicken bouillon cubes
2 teaspoons dried parsley
1/2 teaspoon each dried tarragon, thyme and oregano
1/2 teaspoon salt
1/4 teaspoon pepper

Method:

1. Mix all the ingredients in a 2-quart saucepan. (Use hot water to decrease cooking time.)
2. Cook according to package directions. Stir to fluff.

Approx Per Serving: Cal 174; Prot 4 g; Carbo 38 g; T Fat <1 g; 2% Calories from Fat; Chol <1 mg; Fiber 1 g; Sod 870 mg

Tossed Green Salad with Mandarin Oranges

1 head each red and Bibb lettuce
1/2 (8-ounce) can mandarin oranges, drained
1/2 medium purple onion, thinly sliced
2 tablespoons olive oil
1/4 cup raspberry vinegar
2 teaspoons confectioners' sugar
1/2 teaspoon dry mustard
1 teaspoon poppy seeds

Method:

1. Rinse the lettuce and pat dry with a paper towel. Tear into bite-size pieces and place in a salad bowl. Add the oranges and onion.
2. Combine the olive oil, vinegar, confectioners' sugar, dry mustard and poppy seeds in a blender container or covered jar. Blend or shake until smooth. Add the dressing to the salad and toss to coat.

Approx Per Serving: Cal 121; Prot 2 g; Carbo 12 g; T Fat 8 g; 53% Calories from Fat; Chol 0 mg; Fiber 3 g; Sod 17 mg

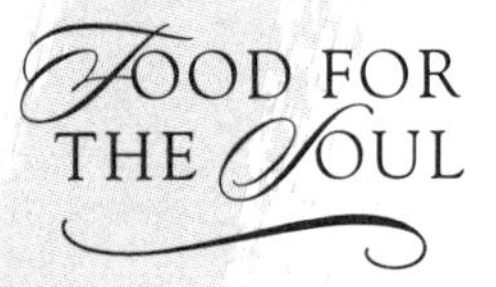

Allow yourself to "putter" now and again and you'll find a broader sense of well-being—of peace.

GREAT GOULASH GATHERING

SIMPLY DELICIOUS GOULASH

PINEAPPLE COLESLAW

HERBED FOCACCIA

SERVES 6

DESSERT SUGGESTION:

Raspberry-Blueberry Whip (page 147)

WINE SUGGESTION:

An Italian varietal on the lighter side, such as Sangiovese. It should be, at most, medium-bodied with a good fruit—zesty, with a light peppery quality.

EN CONCERT:

Begin with cooking the macaroni, brown the ground turkey in a skillet while the macaroni is cooking then mix up the sauce.

GROCERY LIST:

Groceries

1 pound ground fresh turkey breast
1 medium onion *
1 (15-ounce) container marinara sauce
1 (15-ounce) container tomato sauce
1 (12-ounce) package large corkscrew macaroni
1 small head cabbage or 1 package shredded cabbage
1 jar fat-free mayonnaise-type salad dressing
1 bottle Worcestershire sauce *
1 bunch seedless red grapes
1 (8-ounce) can pineapple chunks
1 large focaccia bread round
Fresh basil
Fresh parsley

Staples

Fresh garlic or garlic powder
Salt and pepper
Nonstick vegetable cooking spray
Reduced-fat margarine
Dried parsley and sweet basil

*Note: Staples are items that are usually found in the pantry—look before ordering. An * denotes items that could be considered staples for some families.*

Simply Delicious Goulash

Whether you are coming in from after-school activities or work, there's no place like home, especially when the air is filled with the delicious aroma of home-cooked food and you're starving! Bring out the electric skillet, and supper is ready from beginning to end in less than 45 minutes—and all in one pot!

4 cups uncooked large corkscrew macaroni
1 pound ground fresh turkey breast
1 onion, coarsely chopped
2 cloves of garlic, crushed, or 2 teaspoons garlic powder
1 (15-ounce) container marinara sauce
1 (15-ounce) container tomato sauce
Salt to taste
1/2 teaspoon pepper

Method:

1. Bring a large saucepan of water to a boil. Add the macaroni. Cook for 6 to 8 minutes or until the macaroni is al dente; drain in a colander.
2. While the macaroni is cooking, spray an electric skillet or large skillet generously with nonstick vegetable cooking spray. Heat the skillet until hot.
3. Add the turkey to the skillet. Cook for 4 minutes, stirring constantly with a wooden spoon. Add the onion and garlic. Cook for 6 minutes longer or until the turkey is light brown and crumbly and the onion is translucent.
4. Add the marinara sauce, tomato sauce, drained macaroni, salt and pepper and mix well. Simmer, covered, over medium-low heat for 10 to 15 minutes.

Approx Per Serving: Cal 422; Prot 21 g; Carbo 67 g; T Fat 8 g; 18% Calories from Fat; Chol 45 mg; Fiber 3 g; Sod 934 mg

Tip: *Freeze leftovers in a microwave-safe dish. Microwave on Defrost (30%) to thaw. Let stand for 10 minutes and stir. Microwave on Medium-High (70%) until warm, stirring 2 or 3 times. Microwave on High (100%) just until heated through.*

Work is not always required... Give yourself the gift of sacred idleness, the cultivation of which is now fearfully neglected.

—George MacDonald

REWARD YOURSELF BY ENJOYING WHAT YOU HAVE WORKED SO HARD TO CREATE.

PINEAPPLE COLESLAW

"Cole" is the Old English word for cabbage. If you buy a package of shredded cabbage, your salad will be ready to chill in record time. The tasty fat-free dressing is the secret to this old-fashioned slaw on the lighter side. To prepare, combine 3 cups pre-cut cabbage (or 1 small head fresh cabbage), one 8-ounce can undrained pineapple chunks and 1/2 cup seedless red grapes cut into halves in a 2-quart salad bowl. Add 1/4 cup fat-free salad dressing and mix gently. Chill, covered, until serving time.

Approx Per Serving: Cal 49; Prot 1 g; Carbo 13 g; T Fat <1 g; 3% Calories from Fat; Chol 0 mg; Fiber 1 g; Sod 157 mg

HERBED FOCACCIA

This very popular bread can be prepared in many delicious ways. It is filling, low in calories, and a great alternative to our usual fare. This herbed version is simple and oh, so good! Enjoy!

1 large round focaccia bread
1 1/2 tablespoons reduced-fat margarine, melted
1 teaspoon dried parsley flakes, or 2 teaspoons finely chopped fresh parsley
1/2 teaspoon dried sweet basil, or 1 teaspoon finely chopped fresh basil
1 clove of garlic, crushed, or 1/4 teaspoon garlic powder
1/2 teaspoon Worcestershire sauce

METHOD:

1. Preheat the oven or toaster oven to 400 degrees. Slice the focaccia into 6 wedges.
2. Combine the margarine, parsley flakes, dried basil, garlic and Worcestershire sauce in a bowl and mix well. Spread on the bread wedges.
3. Arrange the wedges on a baking sheet lined with foil. Bake for 5 to 6 minutes or until hot and crisp. Serve hot.

Approx Per Serving: Cal 249; Prot 5 g; Carbo 38 g; T Fat 7 g; 27% Calories from Fat; Chol 0 mg; Fiber <1 g; Sod 480 mg

Tip: *If you are in a hurry, try oven-ready tomato focaccia; warm in the same manner.*

CHICKEN DIVAN

ORANGE AND GRAPEFRUIT SALAD WITH HONEY LEMON DRESSING

FRENCH BREAD (PAGE 53)

SERVES 6

DESSERT SUGGESTION:

Blueberry Tapioca Pudding (page 141)

WINE SUGGESTION:

Pinot Grigio would be an excellent choice. It needs to be a light-bodied, well-balanced white wine with a well-balanced fruit and very little oak. It should have a bright acid to contrast with the richness of the sauce.

EN CONCERT SEQUENCE:

Prepare the chicken in advance, if desired, or prepare the sauce for the chicken while the chicken and broccoli are cooking. Make the salad dressing and prepare the salad while the Divan cooks.

GROCERY LIST:

Groceries

- 3 1/2 pounds boneless skinless chicken breasts
- 1 bunch fresh broccoli
- 8 ounces shredded fat-free Cheddar cheese *
- 1 (2-ounce) jar pimento
- 1 quart skim milk *
- 1 small jar low-fat mayonnaise
- 1 (10-ounce) can light cream of chicken soup
- 2 large navel oranges and 1 large grapefruit
- 1 jar honey *
- 1 (6-ounce) can frozen lemonade concentrate
- 1 head Bibb lettuce
- 1 loaf French bread
- 8 ounces fat-free cream cheese *
- 1 bunch green onions

Staples

- Celery salt, onion salt and curry powder
- Seasoned bread crumbs
- Lemon juice
- Celery seeds
- Fresh garlic

*Note: Staples are items that are usually found in the pantry—look before ordering. An * denotes items that could be considered staples for some families.*

YOU CANNOT OVERCOME A FEAR BY PRETENDING YOU DON'T HAVE IT. YOU CAN BE RID OF IT BY INVOKING THE POWERFUL FORCE OF FAITH TO DISPLACE IT.

—Peale Center for Christian Living

CHICKEN DIVAN

Call them casseroles or main dish specials, but whatever the name, simply delicious one-dish meals can be real winners! Chicken Divan has been a feature in many an elegant restaurant for its eye appeal and scrumptious flavor. I guarantee raves at home too! This version allows you to enjoy all the goodness and still be on the lighter side.

3 1/2 pounds boneless skinless chicken breasts
1/2 teaspoon each celery salt and onion salt
1 bunch fresh broccoli
1 (10-ounce) can light cream of chicken soup
1/2 cup low-fat mayonnaise
1/4 cup skim milk
1 teaspoon lemon juice
1/2 teaspoon curry powder
1/4 cup seasoned bread crumbs
1 tablespoon chopped pimento
1/2 cup shredded fat-free Cheddar cheese

MICROWAVE METHOD:

1. Arrange the chicken in a 2-quart microwave-safe dish, placing the thicker parts toward the outside of the dish. Sprinkle with celery salt and onion salt. Microwave, covered, on High (100%) for 3 to 4 minutes per pound or until the chicken is fork tender and the juices run clear. Slice the chicken diagonally into bite-size pieces.
2. Cut the broccoli into spears with 1/2-inch stems. Combine with 2 tablespoons water in a 1-quart microwave-safe dish with a lid. Microwave, covered, on High (100%) for 4 to 5 minutes or until tender-crisp. Let stand, covered loosely, to preserve the green color.
3. For the sauce, combine the soup, mayonnaise, skim milk, lemon juice and curry powder in a bowl and mix well.
4. Arrange the broccoli in a shallow 2-quart microwave-safe dish, placing the florets toward the outside of the dish. Sprinkle the chicken down the center of the dish. Pour the sauce over the chicken and sprinkle with the bread crumbs and pimento.
5. Cover with plastic wrap, venting one corner. Microwave on Medium-High (70%) for 8 to 10 minutes or until bubbly. Sprinkle with the cheese. Let stand until the cheese melts.

Tip: *You may substitute two 10-ounce packages of frozen broccoli for the fresh broccoli. Remove any foil cover and pierce the wrapping with a fork. Microwave in the package on High (100%) for 8 minutes. Avoid steam when unwrapping.*

Conventional Method:

1. Cut the chicken breasts into halves. Place in a large nonstick skillet and add cold water to cover. Sprinkle with the celery salt and onion salt. Bring to a boil over high heat; cover and reduce the heat.
2. Simmer for 15 minutes or until cooked through. Remove from the liquid to cool. Slice diagonally into bite-size pieces.
3. Cut the broccoli into spears with 1/2-inch stems. Combine with 1/2 cup water in a 1-quart saucepan. Cook just until barely fork tender.
4. Make the sauce and assemble the casserole in a baking dish as in Microwave Method Steps 3 and 4 on page 62. Sprinkle with the cheese.
5. Preheat the oven to 350 degrees. Bake the casserole, covered with foil, for 25 to 30 minutes or until bubbly.

Approx Per Serving: Cal 442; Prot 61 g; Carbo 16 g; T Fat 10 g; 27% Calories from Fat; Chol 166 mg; Fiber 2 g; Sod 879 mg

Orange and Grapefruit Salad with Honey Lemon Dressing

1/3 cup honey
1/3 cup thawed frozen lemonade concentrate
1 teaspoon celery seeds
1 head Bibb lettuce
Sections of 2 large fresh navel oranges
Sections of 1 large grapefruit

Method:

1. For the dressing, process the honey, lemonade concentrate and celery seeds in a blender or food processor container until smooth.
2. Rinse the lettuce leaves and pat dry with paper towels. Arrange 2 leaves on each salad plate.
3. Arrange the orange sections and grapefruit sections alternately on each plate. Drizzle with the dressing.
4. Chill until serving time.

Approx Per Serving: Cal 135; Prot 1 g; Carbo 35 g; T Fat <1 g; 2% Calories from Fat; Chol 0 mg; Fiber 2 g; Sod 4 mg

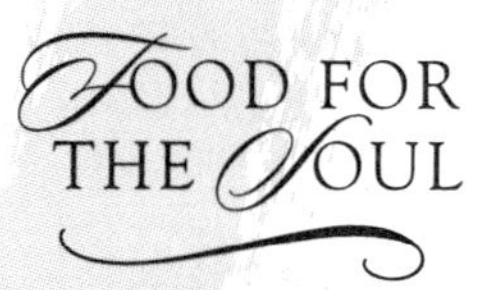

Every one of us needs to learn the art of getting along well with other people. When differences arise, do something about them quickly. There is something in human nature that seems to delight in magnifying differences when they arise. Settle them and get down to the unity between oneself and others.

—Peale Center for Christian Living

VEGETABLE KASHA

GREEN GRAPE AND PINEAPPLE SALAD

ITALIAN BREAD

SERVES 6

DESSERT SUGGESTION:

Angel Food Cake with Peach Sauce (page 132)

WINE SUGGESTION:

A Pinot Blanc or Chardonnay will add a creaminess to the kasha and will not be overpowered by the fruit salad.

EN CONCERT:

Micro-cook the kasha (it stays fluffier) while you prepare the vegetables in a wok or skillet.

GROCERY LIST:

Groceries

1 package kasha
1 (10-ounce) can chicken broth
1 bunch celery *
1 red bell pepper
1 green bell pepper
5 mushrooms
8 ounces pea pods
2 small zucchini
1 bottle teriyaki sauce *
1 (8-ounce) can water chestnuts
1 green onion *
1 loaf Italian bread
1 fresh pineapple
1 pound fresh seedless green grapes

Staples

Olive oil
Fresh garlic or garlic powder
Nonstick vegetable cooking spray
Extra-low-fat corn oil spread

*Note: Staples are items that are usually found in the pantry—look before ordering. An * denotes items that could be considered staples for some families.*

Vegetable Kasha

Seven whole grains and sesame seeds make up this versatile rice-like dish. Full of goodness and savory fresh vegetables, it passes as a complete meal. Make it ahead or in mere minutes. You may substitute five cups of your favorite vegetables such as bean sprouts or broccoli for the ones suggested here.

1 (10-ounce) can chicken broth
3 cups (1 packet) uncooked kasha
1 tablespoon olive oil
2 cloves of garlic, crushed
1 large stalk celery, chopped
1 cup each pea pods, chopped red bell pepper, chopped green bell pepper, chopped zucchini and sliced mushrooms
1 (8-ounce) can sliced water chestnuts, drained
3 tablespoons teriyaki sauce

En Concert Method (Microwave and Conventional):

1. Combine the chicken broth with enough water to measure 2 cups. Place in a microwave-safe dish with a lid. Microwave on High (100%) for 5 minutes.
2. Stir in the kasha. Microwave, covered, on Medium-High (70%) for 15 to 20 minutes, stirring twice. Microwave, uncovered, on High (100%) for 2 minutes longer; stir.
3. Spray a wok or skillet generously with nonstick vegetable cooking spray. Add the olive oil and heat over medium-high heat. Add the garlic, celery, pea pods, bell peppers, zucchini, mushrooms and water chestnuts. Stir-fry until tender.
4. Add the teriyaki sauce and cooked kasha. Turn off the heat and let stand, covered, for 5 minutes. Serve immediately.

Conventional Method:

1. Prepare the chicken stock as in En Concert Method Step 1 and bring to a boil in a 2-quart saucepan. Add the kasha, reduce the heat to medium and cover tightly. Steam for 25 minutes or until liquid is absorbed, stirring twice.
2. Follow En Concert Method Steps 3 and 4.

Approx Per Serving: Cal 163; Prot 7 g; Carbo 29 g; T Fat 4 g; 19% Calories from Fat; Chol <1 mg; Fiber 6 g; Sod 659 mg

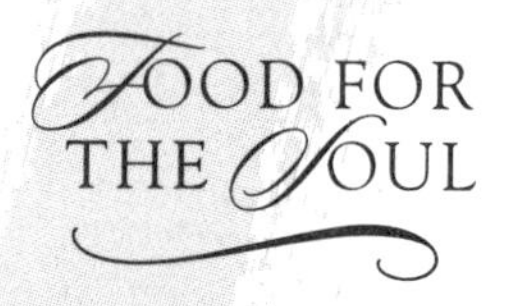

The happiness of your life depends upon the quality of your thoughts. Think positive thoughts!

—*Anonymous*

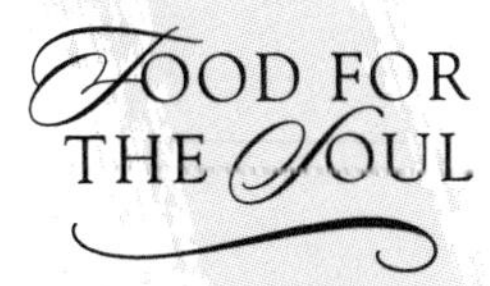

I think we would be able to live in this world more peaceably if our spirituality were to come from looking not just into infinity but very closely at the world—and appreciating its depth and divinity.

—*Thomas Moore, Ph.D.*

Green Grape and Pineapple Salad

Many adjectives are used to describe the adaptable and refreshing green grape. The sweet-tart flavor partnered with fresh pineapple creates a pleasing contrast to the full-bodied Vegetable Kasha.

1 fresh pineapple
1 pound fresh seedless green grapes, chilled

Method:

1. Peel the pineapple and cut into small chunks, discarding the core.
2. Toss the grapes and pineapple chunks together in a medium bowl. Spoon into individual serving bowls.

Approx Per Serving: Cal 92; Prot 1 g; Carbo 23 g; T Fat 1 g; 7% Calories from Fat; Chol 0 mg; Fiber 2 g; Sod 2 mg

Italian Bread

This delicious bread boasts of virtually no fat. In big slices, it gives the impression of indulgence! Combine 2 tablespoons softened extra-low-fat corn oil spread, 1 crushed clove of garlic (or 1/2 teaspoon garlic powder) and 1 minced green onion in a small bowl and mix well. Spread this tasty mixture over 6 (1-inch) thick slices Italian bread and feel guilt free! Place the prepared slices on a baking sheet and bake in a preheated 425-degree oven for 8 to 10 minutes. Serve hot.

Approx Per Serving: Cal 117; Prot 3 g; Carbo 15 g; T Fat 5 g; 38% Calories from Fat; Chol 0 mg; Fiber 1 g; Sod 227 mg

Tempting Turkey Luncheon

QUICK TURKEY QUICHE

CRANBERRY SQUASH

SALAD GREENS AND ARTICHOKE HEARTS

SERVES 6

DESSERT SUGGESTION:

Strawberry sorbet

WINE SUGGESTION:

Select a Sauvignon Blanc or Gewürztraminer with vibrant floral tones to complement the quiche.

EN CONCERT SEQUENCE:

Begin by preparing the stuffing crust. Put the quiche together and micro-cook while preparing the squash. Micro-cook the squash as the quiche stands loosely covered with foil. Prepare the salad as the squash cooks.

GROCERY LIST:

Groceries

1 (6-ounce) package bread stuffing mix
1 package fresh broccoli florets
1 small bunch celery *
1 bunch green onions *
1/3 pound cooked turkey breast
1 (8-ounce) container fat-free sour cream *
4 ounces shredded fat-free Cheddar cheese
2 ounces shredded low-fat Monterey Jack cheese
1 bunch fresh parsley *
2 medium acorn squash
1 small can cranberry sauce
1 (12-ounce) package prepared salad greens
1 bottle low-fat Italian salad dressing *
1 (14-ounce) can artichoke hearts
Pecans

Staples

Reduced-fat margarine
3 eggs
Butter substitute (i.e., Molly McButter)
Salt and pepper

*Note: Staples are items that are usually found in the pantry—look before ordering. An * denotes items that could be considered staples for some families.*

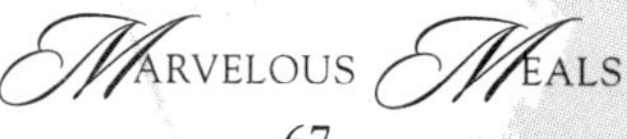

It's only when we truly know and understand that we have a limited time on earth— and that we have no way of knowing when our time is up— that we will begin to live each day to the fullest, as if it was the only one we had.

—Helen Kubler-Ross

Quick Turkey Quiche

This delicious quiche recipe was developed in the heyday of microwave cooking classes to illustrate the ease of using holiday leftovers AND the microwave. Now we enjoy it on the lighter side; teamed with a green salad and delicious squash, dinner is served in a flash! Bon appetit!

1 (6-ounce) package bread stuffing mix
1 tablespoon reduced-fat margarine
1 cup chopped broccoli florets
1 stalk celery, finely chopped
1 cup shredded fat-free Cheddar cheese
1/2 cup shredded low-fat Monterey Jack cheese
1/3 pound chopped cooked turkey breast
2 green onions, sliced into 1/4-inch pieces
1 egg, beaten
2 egg whites, beaten
1 cup fat-free sour cream
1/4 cup chopped parsley

Microwave Method:

1. Combine the contents of the seasoning packet from the stuffing mix with the margarine and hot water called for in a bowl.
2. Add the stuffing mix and mix well. Press into a 10-inch microwave-safe quiche plate or pie plate. Cover with waxed paper. Microwave on High (100%) for 2 minutes.
3. Wrap the broccoli and celery in a nonrecycled white paper towel, forming a pouch. Moisten the pouch with water. Place on a paper plate. Microwave on High (100%) for 2 minutes.
3. While the broccoli and celery are cooking, mix the cheeses in a small bowl.
4. Layer the turkey, broccoli and celery mixture, half the cheese and the green onions in the prepared quiche plate.
5. Combine the egg and egg whites in a bowl and mix well. Fold in the sour cream. Pour over the quiche layers. Sprinkle with the remaining cheese and parsley.
6. Microwave on Medium-High (70%) for 8 to 12 minutes or until the center is partially set. Let stand, covered, for 5 minutes. Cut into wedges to serve.

Conventional Method:

1. Preheat the oven to 350 degrees.
2. Combine the contents of the seasoning packet from the stuffing mix with the margarine and water called for in a medium saucepan. Heat until hot. Add the stuffing mix and stir until the water is absorbed; fluff with a fork. Press lightly into a 10-inch quiche plate or pie plate.
3. Cook the broccoli and celery in a small amount of water in a saucepan just until tender; drain.
4. Follow Microwave Method Steps 3, 4 and 5. Bake, covered with foil, for 35 to 40 minutes or until barely set. Remove from oven. Let stand, covered, for 10 minutes. Cut into wedges to serve.

Approx Per Serving: Cal 291; Prot 26 g; Carbo 32 g; T Fat 6 g; 19% Calories from Fat; Chol 67 mg; Fiber 2 g; Sod 785 mg

Live this day to the fullest—giving it the best you have and love it!

Salad Greens and Artichoke Hearts

Artichoke hearts are full of nutrition, including vitamins A and C, calcium, and iron. Even canned ones are fat free. Add a few toasted pecans for crunch, and these salad greens are dressed and ready to relish!

12 pecans, halved
1 (12-ounce) package prepared salad greens
1 (14-ounce) can artichoke hearts, drained
1/3 cup low-fat Italian salad dressing

Method:

1. Spread the pecans in a microwave-safe pie plate. Microwave on High (100%) for 2 to 4 minutes or until toasted; cool.
2. Rinse the salad greens and roll up between paper towels. Chill in a sealable plastic bag in the refrigerator.
3. Combine the greens with the artichoke hearts in a salad bowl. Add the toasted pecans and toss to mix. Add the salad dressing at serving time.

Approx Per Serving: Cal 65; Prot 2 g; Carbo 6 g; T Fat 4 g; 49% Calories from Fat; Chol 1 mg; Fiber 1 g; Sod 335 mg

Tip: *If you are in a hurry, chill the greens, covered, in the freezer for 10 to 15 minutes. Do not chill for a longer amount of time or they will freeze.*

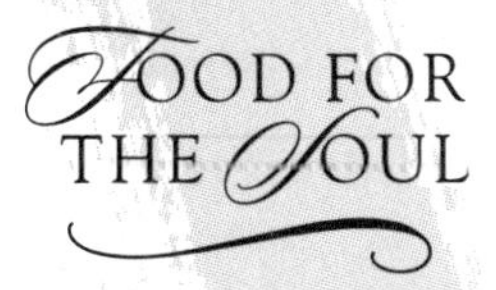

FOOD FOR THE SOUL

THE WORD "ENTHUSIASM" FROM THE GREEK "ENTHEOS" MEANS GOD IN YOU OR FULL OF GOD. WHEN WE CLAIM THE POWER OF ENTHUSIASM TO WORK MIRACLES IN SOLVING PROBLEMS, WE ARE ACTUALLY SAYING THAT GOD HIMSELF IN YOU SUPPLIES THE WISDOM, COURAGE, STRATEGY, AND FAITH NECESSARY TO DEAL WITH ALL DIFFICULTIES. KEEP YOUR ENTHUSIASM GOING!

—Peale Center for Christian Living

CRANBERRY SQUASH

Fall and squash go together like peas in a pod, but until the microwave, squash could only be cooked if we had at least an hour. Now it's ready in minutes with all of its flavorful taste and color! Try it!

2 medium acorn squash
1/2 cup cranberry sauce
1 tablespoon butter substitute

MICROWAVE METHOD:

1. Rinse each squash and pierce 2 or 3 times with a long-tined fork. Place on a microwave-safe rack. Microwave on High (100%) for 6 to 7 minutes.
2. Cut the squash into halves and scoop out the seeds. Place cut side down in a microwave-safe dish and add 1 tablespoon water. Cover with lid or plastic wrap, venting one end. Microwave for 7 to 10 minutes longer.
3. Place the cranberry sauce in a small microwave-safe custard cup or glass measure. Microwave on High (100%) for 25 seconds.
4. Place the squash cut side up on a serving plate. Sprinkle with the butter substitute and spoon the warmed cranberry sauce into the centers.

CONVENTIONAL METHOD:

1. Place the squash in a baking dish. Bake with the turkey quiche at 350 degrees for 45 to 60 minutes or until tender.
2. Place cranberry sauce in small saucepan. Cook over low heat for a few minutes or until heated through.
3. Sprinkle squash with the butter substitute and fill with warmed cranberry sauce.

Approx Per Serving: Cal 95; Prot 1 g; Carbo 25 g; T Fat <1 g; 2% Calories from Fat; Chol <1 mg; Fiber 2 g; Sod 21 mg

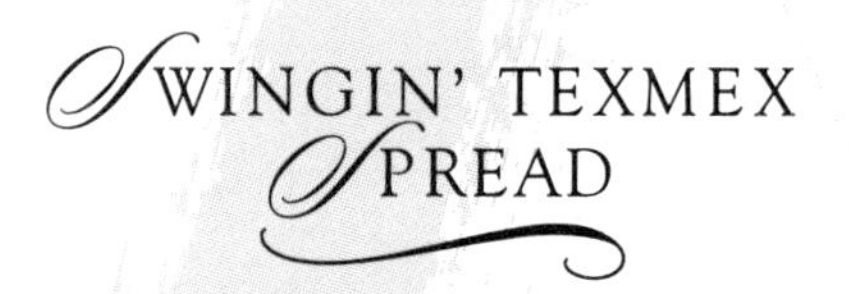

QUICK BEEF BURRITOS

BUTTER LETTUCE SALAD WITH TOASTED PECANS

SERVES 5

DESSERT SUGGESTION:

Instant Strawberry Cake (page 148)

WINE SUGGESTION:

Wine with a fruity element would go well with the spicy element of the burritos. California Gamay, maybe even slightly chilled, would be a good choice.

EN CONCERT:

Mix sauce for burritos and micro-cook. Heat skillet and brown meat and onion. Micro-cook pecans for salad.

GROCERY LIST:

Groceries

1 (28-ounce) can tomatoes
1 (6-ounce) can tomato paste
1 green bell pepper
1 small onion
2 pounds extra-lean ground beef
8 ounces fat-free Cheddar cheese
10 flour tortillas
1/2 cup fat-free sour cream
1 small package pecan halves
2 small heads butter lettuce
1 bottle balsamic vinegar *

Staples

Chili powder, cumin and salt
Olive oil
Sugar
Dry or prepared Dijon mustard
Nonstick vegetable cooking spray

*Note: Staples are items that are usually found in the pantry—look before ordering. An * denotes items that could be considered staples for some families.*

COMPROMISE, IF NOT THE SPICE OF LIFE, IS ITS SOLIDITY.

—Phyllis McKinley

QUICK BEEF BURRITOS

1 (28-ounce) can tomatoes
1 (6-ounce) can tomato paste
2 tablespoons chopped green bell pepper
1 teaspoon chili powder
1/2 teaspoon cumin
1/2 teaspoon salt
2 pounds extra-lean ground beef
1 small onion, chopped
2 cups shredded fat-free Cheddar cheese
10 flour tortillas
1/2 cup fat-free sour cream

EN CONCERT METHOD (MICROWAVE AND CONVENTIONAL):

1. Chop the tomatoes, reserving the juice. Combine the tomatoes and juice, tomato paste, green pepper, chili powder, cumin and salt in a 1-quart microwave-safe bowl with a lid. Microwave, covered, on High (100%) for 6 to 8 minutes, stirring twice.
2. While the tomato mixture is cooking, heat a large skillet sprayed with nonstick vegetable cooking spray. Add the ground beef and onion. Cook for 12 to 15 minutes or until light brown, stirring until the ground beef is crumbly; drain.
3. Stir 1 cup of the tomato mixture into the ground beef. Cook over low heat for 3 minutes longer. Stir in 1/2 cup of the cheese.
4. Spoon the beef mixture down the centers of the tortillas. Fold the sides over, overlapping 1 side; secure with wooden picks.
5. Place seam side up in two 7x11-inch microwave-safe dishes. Spoon the remaining tomato mixture evenly over each tortilla. Cover with heavy plastic wrap, venting one corner.
6. Microwave on Medium-High (70%) for 8 to 10 minutes or until heated through. Sprinkle with the remaining cheese. Microwave for 1 minute longer.
7. Place 2 burritos on each serving plate. Top with sour cream.

Conventional Method:

1. Preheat the oven to 350 degrees.
2. Mix the first 6 ingredients in a saucepan. Simmer over medium-low heat for 15 to 20 minutes or until of the desired consistency.
3. Follow En Concert Method Steps 2, 3 and 4.
4. Place the filled tortillas in a 9x13-inch baking dish sprayed with nonstick vegetable cooking spray. Spoon the remaining tomato mixture evenly over the tortillas. Sprinkle with the remaining cheese. Cover with foil.
5. Bake for 12 to 15 minutes or until the tortillas are heated through and the cheese melts. Serve as in the En Concert Method.

Approx Per Serving: Cal 569; Prot 58 g; Carbo 51 g; T Fat 16 g; 25% Calories from Fat; Chol 77 mg; Fiber 3 g; Sod 1340 mg

Butter Lettuce Salad with Toasted Pecans

Toasted pecans, with their robust flavor and delightful crunch, add personality to this salad.

12 pecan halves
2 small heads butter lettuce
1/4 cup balsamic vinegar
1/2 teaspoon dry mustard, or 1 teaspoon prepared Dijon mustard
1 tablespoon olive oil
1/2 teaspoon sugar

Method:

1. Place the pecans in a microwave-safe pie plate. Microwave on High (100%) for 2 1/2 to 3 minutes; cool.
2. Wash the lettuce and place in ice water to crisp until serving time.
3. Combine the vinegar, dry mustard, olive oil and sugar in a blender container or 2-cup glass measure. Blend or stir until well mixed.
4. Pat the lettuce dry with paper towels and tear into bite-size pieces in a salad bowl. Toss the dressing and pecans with the lettuce.

Approx Per Serving: Cal 73; Prot 1 g; Carbo 5 g; T Fat 6 g; 68% Calories from Fat; Chol 0 mg; Fiber 1 g; Sod 6 mg

You can't experience the truth of another person without feeling love. Understanding and love go together. When we nourish the soul, we automatically nourish our capacity to love another person.

—Jacob Needleman

Cold Weather Comfort

QUICK AND TASTY MEAT LOAF

BAKED POTATOES WITH SOUR CREAM

GINGERED BABY CARROTS

SALAD GREENS WITH TOASTED PECANS

SERVES 4

Dessert Suggestion:

Cranberry-Apple Crisp (page 143)

Wine Suggestion:

A soft, almost sweet, Merlot will go well with this menu. It should be on the lighter side so as not to overpower the subtle flavors in the meat loaf.

En Concert Sequence:

The secret to the success of this delicious old-fashioned comfort food menu is the cooking sequence: potatoes first, meat loaf next, and lastly the carrots. Keep all dishes covered in a 200-degree conventional oven until time to serve.

Grocery List:

Groceries

- 1 pound extra-lean ground beef
- 1 green bell pepper
- 1 carton egg substitute
- 4 medium (5-ounce) baking potatoes
- 1 (8-ounce) container fat-free sour cream
- 1 bunch chopped chives or green onions
- 1 (12-ounce) package baby carrots
- 1 (12-ounce) package prepared salad greens
- Dry onion soup mix *

Staples

- Sugar
- Brown sugar
- Garlic salt or garlic powder
- Seasoned bread crumbs or cracker crumbs
- Skim milk
- Orange juice
- Butter substitute
- Worcestershire sauce
- Ground or fresh ginger
- Catsup
- Pecans
- Dry mustard
- Balsamic vinegar
- Olive oil
- Nonstick vegetable cooking spray

*Note: Staples are items that are usually found in the pantry—look before ordering. An * denotes items that could be considered staples for some families.*

Quick and Tasty Meat Loaf

This all-time favorite recipe has all the flavor of Grandma's without the high fat content. Get daring and try it in the microwave. I haven't baked a meat loaf by the conventional method in over fifteen years!

1 pound extra-lean ground beef
1/2 envelope onion soup mix
1/4 cup egg substitute
1/2 cup seasoned bread crumbs or fine cracker crumbs
1 teaspoon Worcestershire sauce
2 tablespoons skim milk
1/3 teaspoon garlic salt or garlic powder
1/3 cup catsup
3 green bell pepper rings

Microwave Method:

1. Combine the ground beef, onion soup mix, egg substitute, bread crumbs, Worcestershire sauce, skim milk and garlic salt in a medium bowl and mix well. Press into a microwave-safe 4x8 1/2-inch loaf dish or round 1 1/2-quart dish, patting the top flat.
2. Make 3 diagonal indentations on the top with a knife handle or wooden spoon. Spoon the catsup into the indentations. Press the green pepper rings beside each indentation.
3. Microwave on High (100%) for 10 to 12 minutes or until cooked through, rotating the dish after 6 minutes. Let stand, covered, for 5 minutes. Slice to serve.

Conventional Method:

1. Preheat the oven to 350 degrees. Combine the ingredients as in Microwave Method Step 1.
2. Press into a 4x8 1/2-inch baking pan and decorate the top as in Microwave Method Step 2.
3. Bake for 35 to 45 minutes or until cooked through. Let stand, covered, for 5 minutes. Slice to serve.

Approx Per Serving: Cal 255; Prot 29 g; Carbo 16 g; T Fat 8 g; 29% Calories from Fat; Chol 46 mg; Fiber 1 g; Sod 976 mg

Create your "nest"
of comforts,
a place where
you can retreat
and find solace
after a hectic day
or trying time.

The essence of genius is to know what to overlook.

—*William James*

Baked Potatoes with Sour Cream

4 medium (5-ounce) baking potatoes
1 cup fat-free sour cream
1/4 cup finely chopped chives or green onions

Microwave Method:

1. Rinse the potatoes well and pierce all the way through.
2. Place in the microwave oven (preferably on a rack) with space between each potato. Microwave on High (100%) for 14 to 16 minutes or until slightly firm to the touch but not hard.
3. Mix the sour cream and chopped chives in a small bowl.
4. Wrap the potatoes in a paper towel to keep them more crisp, and let stand for up to 20 minutes. Open with a fork and top with the sour cream mixture.

En Concert Method (Microwave and Conventional):

1. Preheat the oven to 450 degrees.
2. Rinse the potatoes well and pierce all the way through in one place. Microwave the potatoes on High (100%) for 12 to 14 minutes.
3. Bake in conventional oven for 5 to 8 minutes or until the skins are crisp.
4. Follow Microwave Method Steps 3 and 4.

Conventional Method:

1. Preheat the oven to 350 degrees.
2. Rinse the potatoes and rub with nonstick cooking spray.
3. Place the potatoes on the middle oven rack and bake for 45 to 50 minutes or until tender. Let stand for several minutes.
4. Follow Microwave Method Step 3. Open the potatoes and top with the sour cream mixture.

Approx Per Serving: Cal 196; Prot 7 g; Carbo 41 g; T Fat <1 g; 1% Calories from Fat; Chol 5 mg; Fiber 3 g; Sod 59 mg

Gingered Baby Carrots

Carrots add both sparkle and texture to any menu, but most importantly, they supply us with one of the essential antioxidants, beta carotene.

1 (12-ounce) package baby carrots
1 tablespoon orange juice
1 teaspoon butter substitute
1/4 teaspoon ground ginger, or 1/2 teaspoon grated fresh ginger
1 teaspoon brown sugar

Microwave Method:

1. Combine the carrots, orange juice, butter substitute, ground ginger and brown sugar in a microwave-safe 1 1/2 quart dish with a lid.
2. Microwave on High (100%) for 7 to 8 minutes or until tender-crisp.

Conventional Method:

1. Combine the carrots with 1/3 cup water in a 1 1/2-quart saucepan. Cook until tender-crisp; drain.
2. Add the remaining ingredients and mix well. Cook over medium heat for 2 minutes longer.

Approx Per Serving: Cal 43; Prot 1 g; Carbo 10 g; T Fat <1 g; 3% Calories from Fat; Chol <1 mg; Fiber 2 g; Sod 45 mg

Salad Greens with Toasted Pecans

For a variation of the salad recipe found on page 73, try substituting salad greens for the butter lettuce. The crisp greens and toasted pecans provide a delightful accompaniment to the sweet-tart smack of the balsamic vinegar.

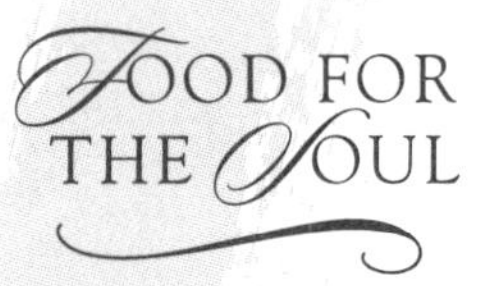

The real test in golf, and in life, is not keeping out of the rough, but in getting out after we're in.

—*John Moore*

LAZY LASAGNA WEEKEND

LASAGNA AL FORNO SPECIAL

CUCUMBER VINAIGRETTE

GARLIC STICKS

SERVES 4

DESSERT SUGGESTION:

Mom's Apple Pie, En Concert (page 138)

WINE SUGGESTION:

Select a fruity bright red such as chianti, Rhône, Syrah, or Zinfandel. Experiment with an Australian Shiraz, or a lighter red wine from South America would be fun, too!

EN CONCERT:

Cook the noodles while toasting the sunflower seeds in the microwave per directions and mix up the sauce. Mix up the vinaigrette and pour over salad and let stand at room temperature while the lasagna cooks.

GROCERY LIST:

Groceries

24 ounces (3 cups) prepared marinara sauce
1/2 cup sunflower seeds
1 (12-ounce) package fresh spinach
1 (8-ounce) package shredded part skim mozzarella cheese
1 small piece fresh Parmesan cheese
1/2 pint 1% cottage cheese
12 ounces fresh whole wheat lasagna noodles, or 1 package dried
1 large cucumber
1 purple onion *
1 pint cherry tomatoes
1 package garlic breadsticks
Fresh garlic *

Staples

Garlic powder, dried oregano and sweet basil
Herb vinegar
Light virgin olive oil
Sugar
Butter-flavor nonstick vegetable cooking spray

*Note: Staples are items that are usually found in the pantry—look before ordering. An * denotes items that could be considered staples for some families.*

Lasagna al Forno Special

It is said that on Christmas Eve the Italian grandmother measures the size of the grandchildren's mouths to determine the size of the noodles! Although we seldom make our own noodles, there are many places to buy fresh pasta now. It is more tasty and requires no precooking!

12 ounces fresh whole wheat lasagna noodles, or 12 ounces dried
1/2 cup sunflower seeds
1 clove of garlic, crushed
1/2 teaspoon each oregano and sweet basil
3 cups marinara sauce
1 (12-ounce) package fresh spinach, torn into bite-size pieces
1 (8-ounce) package shredded part-skim mozzarella cheese
1/4 cup grated fresh Parmesan cheese (optional)
1 cup 1% cottage cheese

Microwave Method:

1. Cut fresh noodles to the size of a 3-quart microwave-safe dish, or cook dried noodles in boiling salted water in a large saucepan for 8 to 10 minutes or until tender and drain.
2. Spread the sunflower seeds in a microwave-safe pie plate. Microwave on High (100%) for 4 to 6 minutes or until toasted.
3. Mix the next 3 ingredients with marinara sauce in a bowl.
4. Spread 3/4 cup of the marinara mixture in the 3-quart dish. Alternate layers of the noodles, spinach, marinara mixture, cottage cheese, sunflower seeds and mozzarella cheese in the dish until all ingredients are used, ending with the marinara mixture. Sprinkle with the Parmesan cheese.
5. Microwave on Medium-High (70%) for 8 to 10 minutes or until heated through.

En Concert Method
(Microwave and Conventional):

1. Preheat the oven to 350 degrees. Follow Microwave Method Steps 1, 2, 3 and 4.
2. Bake for 25 to 35 minutes or until heated through.

Approx Per Serving: Cal 686; Prot 39 g; Carbo 81 g; T Fat 28 g; 35% Calories from Fat; Chol 36 mg; Fiber 10 g; Sod 1669 mg

You don't get to choose how you're going to die, or when. You can only decide how you're going to live. Now!

—Joan Baez

I AM ONLY ONE, BUT STILL I AM ONE. I CANNOT DO EVERYTHING, BUT STILL I CAN DO SOMETHING; AND BECAUSE I CANNOT DO EVERYTHING, I WILL NOT REFUSE TO DO THE SOMETHING THAT I CAN DO.

—Edward Everett Hale

Cucumber Vinaigrette

The fresh zippy crunch of this salad is the perfect texture and taste blend to complement the lasagna. It is quick and easy to prepare!

1 large cucumber, chilled
1/4 purple onion, thinly sliced
5 cherry tomatoes, cut into halves
1/4 cup herb vinegar
1/2 teaspoon sugar
2 tablespoons light virgin olive oil

Method:

1. Peel the cucumber and slice 1/8 inch thick. Arrange the cucumber slices, sliced onion and cherry tomato halves on a serving platter.
2. Combine the vinegar, sugar and olive oil in a bowl or jar; stir or shake, covered, until well blended.
3. Drizzle the dressing over the salad. Marinate, covered, until serving time.

Approx Per Serving: Cal 83; Prot 1 g; Carbo 6 g; T Fat 7 g; 71% Calories from Fat; Chol 0 mg; Fiber 1 g; Sod 4 mg

Garlic Sticks

These provide the flavor of butter, but without the fat. Go ahead; have several pieces!

1/2 teaspoon crushed dried oregano
2 teaspoons garlic powder
Butter-flavor nonstick vegetable cooking spray
8 garlic breadsticks

Method:

1. Preheat the oven to 425 degrees. Mix the oregano and garlic powder in a small dish. Spread on waxed paper.
2. Spray the nonstick vegetable cooking spray generously over the breadsticks. Roll in the seasonings. Arrange on a baking sheet.
3. Bake for 5 to 10 minutes. Serve hot.

Approx Per Serving: Cal 280; Prot 10 g; Carbo 44 g; T Fat 8 g; 25% Calories from Fat; Chol 0 mg; Fiber 2 g; Sod 580 mg

SAVORY CHILI IN A BREAD BOWL

WILTED SPINACH AND CHEESE SALAD

SWEET-HOT DRESSING

SERVES 8

DESSERT SUGGESTION:

Fruit Kabobs with Chocolate Dip (pages 152–53)

WINE SUGGESTION:

A hearty Zinfandel will be delightful with this menu. It should be weighty enough to complement the chili, yet subtle enough in its finish for the pepper and spices.

EN CONCERT:

Heat skillet and brown the meat and onion while preparing the sauce and pouring into large Dutch oven. Prepare bread bowls as chili simmers. Make up the salad and heat salad dressing at the last minure.

GROCERY LIST:

Groceries

- 2 pounds extra-lean ground beef
- 1 large onion
- 2 (27-ounce) cans red kidney beans
- 1 (16-ounce) can water-pack tomatoes
- 1 (6-ounce) can tomato paste
- 1 cup fresh refrigerated marinara sauce
- 1 bunch fresh parsley
- 1 (8-ounce) container fat-free sour cream
- 8 large French or Kaiser rolls
- 1 pound fresh spinach
- 1 pint fresh strawberries
- 1 pint fresh blueberries
- 4 ounces shredded fat-free Cheddar cheese
- 1 pint cider vinegar *
- 1 quart unsweetened apple juice

Staples

- Chili powder
- Cornstarch
- Brown sugar
- Dijon mustard
- Poppy seeds
- Nonstick vegetable cooking spray

*Note: Staples are items that are usually found in the pantry—look before ordering. An * denotes items that could be considered staples for some families.*

A LITTLE OF

WHAT YOU FANCY

DOES YOU GOOD.

—Marie Lloyd

SAVORY CHILI IN A BREAD BOWL

Sunday afternoon football! Have a party! A chili supper is the perfect answer to an informal party. It is delicious, low in fat—yet hearty—and a great dish to feed a crowd. This recipe is said to have been a winner one year in the popular two-day marathon chili contest held in the little ghost town of Terlinqua, Texas. Make it ahead to get the best flavor blend, then just reheat it and serve!

2 pounds extra-lean ground beef
1 large onion, chopped
2 (27-ounce) cans red kidney beans
1 (16-ounce) can water-pack tomatoes
1 (6-ounce) can tomato paste
1 cup fresh refrigerated marinara sauce
1 1/2 tablespoons chili powder
8 large French or Kaiser rolls
1 bunch fresh parsley
Sour cream to taste

CONVENTIONAL METHOD:

1. Heat a large skillet sprayed with nonstick vegetable cooking spray. Add the ground beef and onion. Cook until light brown, stirring until the ground beef is crumbly; drain.
2. Combine the beans, tomatoes, tomato paste, marinara sauce and chili powder in a large bowl.
3. Pour the tomato mixture into a large saucepan. Add the ground beef mixture and mix well. Bring to a boil and reduce the heat. Simmer for 1 hour.
4. Cut off the tops of the rolls and remove the soft bread from the inside to form bowls. Reserve the bread for another use. Place the bread bowls in a plastic bag until serving time.
5. Preheat the oven to 350 degrees. Place the bread bowls on a baking sheet. Heat in the oven for 6 to 8 minutes.
6. Place the bread bowls on the serving plates and ladle the chili into the centers. Top with a sprig of parsley and a dollop of sour cream.

En Concert Method (Microwave and Conventional):

1. Follow Conventional Method Steps 1 and 2 on page 82. Combine the ground beef mixture and the tomato mixture in a 3-quart microwave-safe bowl and mix well.
2. Microwave on Medium (50%) for 20 to 25 minutes, stirring 3 times.
3. Shape the bread bowls as in Conventional Method Step 4.
4. Microwave the bread bowls 4 at a time on Medium-High (70%) for 25 to 35 seconds or until hot. Place on serving plates and fill with the hot chili. Top with a sprig of parsley and a dollop of sour cream.

Approx Per Serving: Cal 592; Prot 44 g; Carbo 78 g; T Fat 13 g; 19% Calories from Fat; Chol 45 mg; Fiber 17 g; Sod 1615 mg

Wilted Spinach and Cheese Salad

The spicy hot dressing is the key to making this salad a winner. Keep the greens icy cold by tossing a few ice cubes on top until ready to serve.

1 pound fresh spinach
1 cup sliced fresh strawberries
1 cup fresh blueberries
1 cup shredded fat-free Cheddar cheese
1 recipe Sweet-Hot Dressing (page 84)

Method:

1. Remove the stems from the spinach and discard. Wash the leaves and pat dry with paper towels. Tear into bite-size pieces. Chill until serving time.
2. Combine the spinach, strawberries, blueberries and cheese in a large salad bowl. Chill, covered, until serving time.
3. Pour the Sweet-Hot Dressing over the salad and toss gently to mix. Serve immediately.

Approx Per Serving: Cal 98; Prot 6 g; Carbo 17 g; T Fat 1 g; 12% Calories from Fat; Chol 1 mg; Fiber 2 g; Sod 180 mg

If we could see that everything, even tragedy, is a gift in disguise, we would then find the best way to nourish the soul. It is our choice to take the negative or the positive fork in the road when trouble strikes. It is far better to take the positive but much easier to take the negative and allow ourselves to feel victimized by the circumstances.

—Helen Kubler-Ross

WHATEVER YOU DO,

OR DREAM YOU CAN,

BEGIN IT;

BOLDNESS HAS

GENIUS, POWER

AND MAGIC IN IT.

—Johann Wolfgang von Goethe

Sweet-Hot Dressing

This delicious dressing is from Cooking Light *magazine; you will never miss the oil.*

4 teaspoons cornstarch
1/2 cup water
1 1/3 cups unsweetened apple juice
2/3 cup cider vinegar
2 tablespoons brown sugar
2 teaspoons Dijon mustard
2 tablespoons poppy seeds

Microwave Method:

1. Blend the cornstarch and water in a 4-cup glass measure. Stir in the apple juice, vinegar, brown sugar, mustard and poppy seeds.
2. Microwave on High (100%) for 3 to 4 minutes or until the mixture comes to a boil. Microwave for 1 minute longer; stir.
3. Pour hot over salad and serve immediately.

Conventional Method:

1. Blend the cornstarch and water in a small nonaluminum saucepan. Stir in the remaining ingredients.
2. Bring to boil, stirring constantly. Cook for 1 minute longer or until thickened and smooth, stirring constantly.
3. Pour hot over salad and serve immediately.

Approx Per Serving: Cal 54; Prot 1 g; Carbo 11 g; T Fat 1 g; 18% Calories from Fat; Chol 0 mg; Fiber <1 g; Sod 35 mg

ROASTED RED PEPPER PASTA WITH PEAS AND ONIONS

POPEYE'S SALAD

CREAM CHEESE AND HERB BREAD

SERVES 6

DESSERT SUGGESTION:

Waikiki Sundaes (page 154)

WINE SUGGESTION:

Either red or white will work well with this menu. A Cabernet Sauvignon, Merlot, Sauvignon Blanc, or a French-American hybrid such as Vidal or Seyval Blanc—all will complement the sauce and red pepper.

EN CONCERT:

Micro-cook the pecans while the water boils for the pasta. Boil the pasta on the cooktop as you micro-cook the onions and peas. Prepare the cream cheese-herb mixture for the bread.

GROCERY LIST:

Groceries

- $5^1/_2$ cups small shell pasta
- 2 medium onions
- 1 (10-ounce) package frozen green peas without sauce
- 1 (8-ounce) jar roasted red peppers
- 1 small piece Parmesan cheese
- $1^1/_2$ cups shredded fat-free mozzarella cheese
- Fresh parsley
- 2 heads butter lettuce
- 1 (12-ounce) package fresh spinach
- 6 fresh mushrooms
- 3 fresh scallions
- 3 slices bacon
- 1 small bottle fat-free raspberry salad dressing
- 6 crusty French rolls
- 1 (3-ounce) package fat-free cream cheese

Staples

- Reduced-fat margarine
- Salt and coarsely ground pepper
- Olive oil
- Sugar
- Dry mustard or Dijon mustard
- Dried sweet basil or tarragon
- Nonstick vegetable cooking spray

Note: Staples are items that are usually found in the pantry—look before ordering.

LIVING IS A FORM OF NOT BEING SURE, NOT KNOWING WHAT'S NEXT OR HOW... THE ARTIST NEVER ENTIRELY KNOWS. WE GUESS. WE MAY BE WRONG BUT WE TAKE LEAP AFTER LEAP IN THE DARK.

—Agnes De Mille

ROASTED RED PEPPER PASTA WITH PEAS AND ONIONS

All of America is having a love affair with pasta; our consumption went up over 67 percent in the early nineties. The inspiration for this recipe came from the Moosewood Cookbook. *The great news is that it can be delicious without the high-fat cheese. Using the microwave oven en concert with the stove top gets this main dish ready with half the cleanup time. Help yourself to seconds!*

5½ cups uncooked small shell pasta
Salt to taste
2 medium onions, chopped
1 tablespoon reduced-fat margarine
1 (10-ounce) package frozen green peas without sauce
2 tablespoons chopped roasted red peppers
¼ cup grated Parmesan cheese
1½ cups shredded fat-free mozzarella cheese
Coarsely ground pepper to taste
Fresh parsley

EN CONCERT METHOD (MICROWAVE AND CONVENTIONAL):

1. Bring a large saucepan of water to a boil. Add the pasta and salt to taste. Cover and bring to a boil again. Remove the cover and cook for 10 to 12 minutes or until al dente.
2. Combine the onions and margarine in a microwave-safe 3-quart dish with a lid. Microwave, covered, on High (100%) for 3 to 4 minutes or until limp; stir and set aside with cover in place.
3. Place the package of frozen peas on a paper plate in the center of the microwave oven, removing any foil wrapping and piercing plastic pouches. Microwave on High (100%) for 3½ to 4 minutes. Combine with the onions in the covered dish.
4. Drain the pasta. Combine the pasta and roasted red peppers with the peas and onions in a large microwave-safe bowl. Sprinkle with the cheeses, salt and pepper and toss to mix well.
5. Microwave on Medium-High (70%) for 3 minutes. Garnish with fresh parsley.

CONVENTIONAL METHOD:

1. Follow En Concert Method Step 1.
2. Coat a large skillet generously with nonstick vegetable cooking spray and heat until hot. Add the onions and margarine. Cook over medium heat until the onions are tender and light brown, stirring 3 or 4 times.
3. Add the peas to the skillet and mix well. Cook just until the peas are tender. Add the roasted red peppers.
4. Drain the pasta and add to the skillet. Add the cheeses and season with salt and pepper to taste. Simmer, covered, for 10 minutes. Garnish with parsley.

Approx Per Serving: Cal 488; Prot 26 g; Carbo 84 g; T Fat 4 g; 8% Calories from Fat; Chol 6 mg; Fiber 6 g; Sod 451 mg

LET THE ARTIST IN YOU LEAP INTO THE DARK OF SOMETHING YOU BELIEVE IN AND TRUST YOUR INSTINCTS.

CREAM CHEESE AND HERB BREAD

Bread is high in carbohydrates and relatively low in fat and great for producing energy and a chock-full feeling! The key is to select the tastiest rolls you can find, and soon you won't miss the villain of healthy living—butter. If you can't live without the buttery texture, try fat-free cream cheese sprinkled with a dash of finely crushed sweet basil or other favorite herb.

6 crusty French rolls
3 tablespoons fat-free cream cheese, softened
1/8 teaspoon finely crushed sweet basil or tarragon

CONVENTIONAL METHOD:

1. Preheat the oven to 425 degrees. Cut the rolls into halves.
2. Combine the cream cheese and basil or tarragon in a bowl and mix well. Spread on the cut sides of the rolls. Place the halves together and wrap the rolls in foil.
3. Heat for 5 to 8 minutes. Serve immediately.

Approx Per Serving: Cal 108; Prot 5 g; Carbo 20 g; T Fat 1 g; 8% Calories from Fat; Chol 1 mg; Fiber 1 g; Sod 270 mg

A BAD HABIT NEVER DISAPPEARS MIRACULOUSLY; IT'S AN UNDO-IT-YOURSELF PROJECT.

—*Abigail Van Buren*

POPEYE'S SALAD

Popeye was the one who ate spinach when I was a child, and I wasn't too impressed. Try spinach blended with these tasty morsels and reap its vitamin benefits.

3 slices bacon
1 (12-ounce) package fresh spinach
6 fresh mushrooms, sliced
3 fresh scallions, chopped
1/4 cup fat-free raspberry salad dressing

METHOD:

1. Place the bacon between 2 paper towels on a paper plate or microwave-safe plate. Microwave on High (100%) for 2 to 3 minutes. Let stand to cool.
2. Rinse and stem the spinach and pat dry with paper towels. Tear into bite-size pieces in a large salad bowl.
3. Add the mushrooms and scallions. Crumble the bacon and add to the salad. Drizzle with the salad dressing and toss to mix. Chill, covered, until serving time.

Approx Per Serving: Cal 50; Prot 3 g; Carbo 6 g; T Fat 2 g; 31% Calories from Fat; Chol 3 mg; Fiber 2 g; Sod 109 mg

LINGUINI PRIMAVERA

MIXED GREENS AND STRAWBERRIES

GARLIC FRENCH ROLLS

SERVES 4

DESSERT SUGGESTION:

Chocolate Angel Meringues (pages 130–31)

WINE SUGGESTION:

A California Sangiovese or, if a white wine is preferred, a Pinot Grigio will have a nice crisp edge and show off the pasta.

EN CONCERT:

Boil linguini on the cooktop while you micro-cook the vegetables. As linguini micro-cooks, mix up the garlic spread. Make salad and broil garlic bread just before serving.

GROCERY LIST:

Groceries

1 (12-ounce) package enriched egg linguini
1 each red, yellow and green bell pepper
2 tomatoes
1 medium red onion *
1 small jar prepared pesto
1 small piece fresh Parmesan cheese
12 ounces premixed fresh salad greens
5 fresh strawberries
1 bottle fat-free raspberry salad dressing
4 French bread rolls
Italian parsley for garnish (optional)

Staples

Extra-virgin olive oil
Salt and pepper
Fresh garlic or garlic powder
Red wine vinegar
Sugar
Extra-light corn oil spread
Nonstick vegetable cooking spray

*Note: Staples are items that are usually found in the pantry—look before ordering. An * denotes items that could be considered staples for some families.*

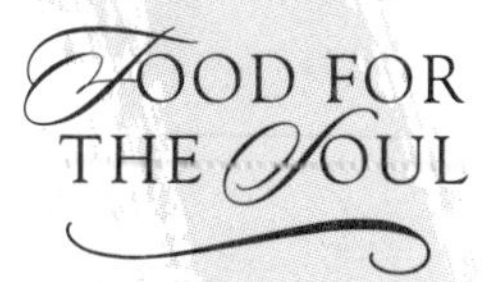

CHARACTER CONTRIBUTES TO BEAUTY. IT FORTIFIES A WOMAN AS HER YOUTH FADES. A MODE OF CONDUCT, A STANDARD OF COURAGE, DISCIPLINE, FORTITUDE AND INTEGRITY CAN DO A GREAT DEAL TO MAKE A WOMAN BEAUTIFUL.

—Jacqueline Bisset

LINGUINI PRIMAVERA

The medley of pastas available creates a banquet of choices. With a little care in our selection of sauces, we can eat to our hearts' content. This gratifying dish will fill you up without filling you out!

12 ounces uncooked enriched egg linguini
1/2 cup each chopped green, red and yellow bell pepper
1 medium red onion, chopped
3 large cloves of garlic, chopped
2 tomatoes, peeled, chopped
1 tablespoon extra-virgin olive oil
1/4 cup red wine vinegar
1/4 cup prepared pesto
Salt and pepper to taste
1/4 cup grated Parmesan cheese

EN CONCERT METHOD:

1. Cook the linguini for 3 to 4 minutes or until al dente using the package directions.
2. Combine the chopped vegetables with the olive oil in a microwave-safe 2-quart dish with a lid. Microwave, covered, on High (100%) for 4 to 5 minutes or until tender but still intact. Add the vinegar and pesto. Microwave for 1 to 2 minutes longer.
3. Drain the linguini and add to the hot vegetables; season with salt and pepper. Microwave on High (100%) for 3 to 4 minutes or until heated through, stirring once. Sprinkle with the cheese. Let stand, covered, for 3 to 5 minutes or until the cheese melts. Garnish with Italian parsley.

CONVENTIONAL METHOD:

1. Follow En Concert Method Step 1. Heat a large skillet sprayed with nonstick vegetable cooking spray. Add chopped vegetables with the olive oil. Cook until tender but not brown.
2. Add the vinegar and pesto. Cook for 5 minutes, stirring frequently. Drain the linguini and add to the sauce; mix gently. Season with salt and pepper. Sprinkle with the cheese. Let stand, covered, for several minutes to melt the cheese. Garnish with Italian parsley.

Approx Per Serving: Cal 495; Prot 18 g; Carbo 75 g; T Fat 14 g; 26% Calories from Fat; Chol 9 mg; Fiber 5 g; Sod 237 mg

Tip: *To save time, do not peel the tomatoes, and chop the bell peppers, onion and garlic in the food processor, taking care not to purée them.*

Mixed Greens and Strawberries

The key to a good green salad is fresh crispy greens. The natural crunch complements the soft texture of the pasta and creates a consummate match. To produce the crispness, as soon as you get home from the grocery, douse greens with cold water, pat dry with a paper towel and chill. If you are going to use them immediately place them in a large salad bowl and toss in a few ice cubes while you prepare the pasta; remember to remove the ice cubes before serving. Fresh crisp greens in seconds!

12 ounces premixed fresh salad greens
5 fresh strawberries, sliced lengthwise
1 teaspoon sugar
1/4 cup fat-free raspberry salad dressing

Method:

1. Combine the greens and strawberries in a large salad bowl. Sprinkle with the sugar.
2. Add the raspberry salad dressing and toss to mix well. Spoon onto chilled salad plates.

Approx Per Serving: Cal 41; Prot 1 g; Carbo 9 g; T Fat <1 g; 6% Calories from Fat; Chol 0 mg; Fiber 2 g; Sod 39 mg

Tip: *To chill salad plates quickly, place them in the freezer for 10 minutes.*

Garlic French Rolls

This toaster oven method is great in the summer. In seconds you'll enjoy soft warm rolls without a hot kitchen!

2 cloves of garlic, crushed, or 2 teaspoons garlic powder
2 tablespoons extra-light corn oil spread, softened
4 French bread rolls

Toaster Oven Method:

1. Mix the garlic with the corn oil spread in a small bowl.
2. Slice the bread rolls into halves and spread with the garlic mixture.
3. Turn the toaster oven to broil. Toast the rolls to golden brown. Serve immediately.

Approx Per Serving: Cal 153; Prot 4 g; Carbo 20 g; T Fat 7 g; 39% Calories from Fat; Chol 0 mg; Fiber 1 g; Sod 307 mg

Remember—
when you point
your finger at
someone else,
three fingers
are pointing
back at you.
The past cannot
be changed,
but the future
is still in
our power.
Forgiveness
is the key to
peace of mind.

—Anonymous

Entertaining Elegantly with Ease

60 Minutes or Less

Menus

Brunch on the Light Side

The Creole Connection

Packing a Picnic

Chutney Chicken Barbecue

A Hen Party

Grilling-Out en Concert

Simply Scrumptious Supper

Wine

Sipping a glass of wine and creating the ambience of peace, serenity and camaraderie is as important as drinking the wine itself.

Enjoying a glass of wine with meals has been a tradition for centuries in homes throughout the world, especially in the Mediterranean regions; yet, the perception that wine is not good for us still exists today. With this in mind, and as a person who thoroughly enjoys a glass of wine with my meal, I asked the organization Women for WineSense, which promotes the appreciation and responsible consumption of wine, to share with us the latest information on the healthy side of wine. Elisabeth Holmgren, the Director of the Research and Education Department of The Wine Institute and chairperson of the Health and Social Issues Committee, shared the following information.

According to scientific research, enjoying wine with dinner may enhance your health. Over a dozen studies now report that moderate alcohol consumption not only reduces the risk of coronary heart disease, but also premature death from all causes, contributing to increased life expectancy for both men and women. Noted alcohol researcher Dr. Arthur Klatsky reported in the American Journal of Cardiology *in 1993 that based on data collected from 82,000 adults in California, moderate wine drinkers faced the lowest risk for heart disease.*

Also, major scientific advancements have been made with the discovery that wines' phenolic compounds behave like antioxidants when absorbed in the bloodstream. One unsolved puzzle is the debate over whether red or white wine provides more phenolic antioxidant power. Most studies conclude that red wine contains more phenolic compounds than white wine. Other studies suggest that the compounds in white wine may actually provide a more potent source.

Thus, the conclusion is to select your favorite wine and enjoy a glass with your meal. With all this good news, we must ask how much should we drink. Here are some important guidelines:

* *Drink a glass of wine* **with** *a meal or with food (i.e. appetizers)*
* *A drink is defined as five ounces of wine. A reasonable guideline would be one and no more than two glasses of wine daily.*
* *Wine is meant to be sipped and enjoyed as a way to make every meal an occasion of peaceful pleasure.*
* *The current philosophy is to select your favorite wine and not worry if it is red or white.*
* *Women for WineSense professionals have selected the best wine pairings for most of the menus in this book. Try their suggestions and enjoy selecting your own.*

Another good alternative is to select one of the several non-alcoholic wines. Some of the latest research has found that many of the same health benefits derived from traditional wines continue to be true when drinking non-alcoholic wine. Recent research studies done at the University of California by enologist Andrew Waterhouse have found that the wine, not the alcohol, is what is good for us. As mentioned above, the heart benefits come from the phenolics; these are the natural antioxidants, which are plentiful in wine after fermentation. Currently there are three wineries featuring non-alcoholic wine: Ariel (which makes only non-alcoholic wines), Sutter Home, and St. Regis. The alcoholic content is only 0.5 percent, compared to traditional wines, which vary from 11 to 14 percent alcohol content.

Sipping a glass of wine and creating the ambience of peace, serenity and camaraderie is as important as drinking the wine itself.
This is an excellent alternative and I recommend enjoying some yourself and certainly having it on hand for guests who do not drink alcohol. The four favorites at our house are: Ariel Napa Vintner's Reserve Cabernet and Reserve Chardonnay, the Sutter Home Fré White Zinfandel, and the St. Regis Blanc. Interestingly, Ariel Vineyards won the 1996–1997 Gold Medal in a blind wine tasting where it competed with alcoholic wines.

Brunch on the Light Side

ORANGE JUICE FIZZ

VEGETABLE AND CHEESE OMELET

HOMEMADE JIFFY HASH BROWNS

APRICOT STREUSEL COFFEE CAKE

SERVES 8

EN CONCERT:

If possible, bake the coffee cake in advance. If not possible, preheat conventional oven, mix up the coffee cake and pop in the oven. As the coffee cake bakes, cook the potatoes and then the omelet according to the *en concert* directions.

GROCERY LIST:

Groceries

1 quart fresh orange juice
1 (24-ounce) bottle ginger ale *
1 bunch fresh mint leaves *
1 small onion
4 large (5-ounce) baking potatoes
1 quart skim milk *
3 cartons egg substitute
1 package baking mix
1 (8-ounce) package shredded fat-free Cheddar cheese *
6 green onions *
1 red bell pepper *
1 green bell pepper *
1 jar apricot preserves *

Staples

Butter substitute
Dried tarragon
Salt and coarsely ground pepper
Ground cinnamon
Sugar
Brown sugar
Nonstick vegetable cooking spray

*Note: Staples are items that are usually found in the pantry—look before ordering. An * denotes items that could be considered staples for some families.*

Orange Juice Fizz

Add a little fizz to a favorite breakfast drink and add pizzazz—and still chalk up wholesome goodness! Or, if you prefer Champagne, substitute one chilled 750-milliliter bottle for the ginger ale.

1 quart freshly squeezed orange juice
2 cups ginger ale
Sprigs of fresh mint

Method:

1. Chill the orange juice and ginger ale in the refrigerator.
2. Combine the orange juice and ginger ale in a chilled pitcher just before serving and mix gently.
3. Serve in glasses with a sprig of mint.

Approx Per Serving: Cal 77; Prot 1 g; Carbo 18 g; T Fat <1 g; 3% Calories from Fat; Chol 0 mg; Fiber <1 g; Sod 6 mg

Homemade Jiffy Hash Browns

Imagine hot tender freshly cooked hash browns in minutes, and you've got it!

4 large baking potatoes, scrubbed
1 small onion, chopped
1/2 teaspoon dried tarragon
1 tablespoon butter substitute
Salt and pepper to taste

En Concert Method (Microwave and Conventional):

1. Pierce the potatoes with a 2-tined fork.
2. Microwave the potatoes on High (100%) for 12 to 15 minutes or until cooked through but still firm. Let stand, wrapped in paper towels, for 5 to 10 minutes. Chop into small pieces.
3. Heat a skillet sprayed with nonstick vegetable cooking spray. Add the potatoes, onion, tarragon and butter substitute. Season with salt and pepper. Cook until golden brown, stirring frequently. Set aside, covered, until serving time.

Approx Per Serving: Cal 107; Prot 2 g; Carbo 25 g; T Fat <1 g; 1% Calories from Fat; Chol <1 mg; Fiber 2 g; Sod 15 mg

The soul should always stand ajar, ready to welcome the ecstatic experience.

—Emily Dickinson

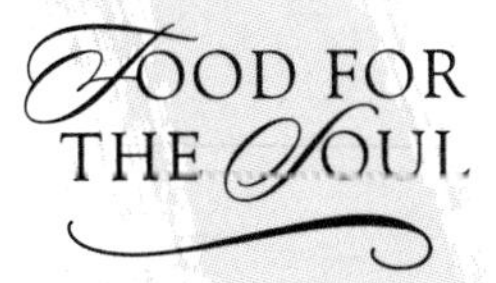

INSIDE MYSELF IS
A PLACE WHERE
I LIVE ALL ALONE
AND THAT'S
WHERE YOU
RENEW YOUR
SPRINGS THAT
NEVER DRY UP.

—Pearl Buck

VEGETABLE AND CHEESE OMELET

You'll be amazed how delicious this omelet will taste. Finely chopped broccoli also makes a tasty addition. It is guiltless, so help yourself to seconds!

6 green onions, finely chopped
6 tablespoons each chopped red and green bell pepper
2 cartons egg substitute, or the equivalent of 8 eggs
2/3 cup skim milk
2 cups shredded fat-free Cheddar cheese
Salt and coarsely ground pepper to taste

EN CONCERT METHOD (MICROWAVE AND CONVENTIONAL):

1. Combine the green onions and bell peppers in a microwave-safe dish or glass measure. Microwave on High (100%) for 2 to 3 minutes or just until tender.
2. Beat the egg substitute and milk together in a bowl.
3. Heat a skillet sprayed with nonstick vegetable cooking spray. Pour in half the egg mixture. Sprinkle half the green onion and pepper mixture and half the cheese over the top. Season with salt and pepper.
4. Cook, covered, over medium-low heat just until set in the center, checking frequently. Loosen the side with a spatula and fold in half. Remove to a plate and cut into 4 serving pieces.
5. Repeat with the remaining ingredients.

CONVENTIONAL METHOD:

1. Spray a skillet with nonstick vegetable cooking spray. Add the green onions, bell peppers and 2 tablespoons water. Cook over medium-high heat just until tender-crisp, stirring frequently.
2. Follow Microwave Method Steps 2, 3, 4 and 5.

Approx Per Serving: Cal 97; Prot 18 g; Carbo 2 g; T Fat 2 g; 18% Calories from Fat; Chol 4 mg; Fiber <1 g; Sod 317 mg

Tip: *Use two skillets at the same time for quicker preparation (or for a crowd).*

APRICOT STREUSEL COFFEE CAKE

A traditional favorite, this lighter version of an old-time family treat is every bit as satisfying, and you can't even tell it's a featherweight!

2 cups baking mix
2/3 cup skim milk
1/4 cup egg substitute, or the equivalent of 1 egg
3 tablespoons sugar
1/2 teaspoon ground cinnamon
1/4 cup apricot preserves
3 tablespoons brown sugar
1/2 teaspoon ground cinnamon

CONVENTIONAL METHOD:

1. Preheat the oven to 350 degrees. Spray a round 9-inch baking pan with nonstick vegetable cooking spray.
2. Combine the baking mix, skim milk, egg substitute, sugar and 1/2 teaspoon cinnamon in a mixer bowl and beat until smooth. Pour evenly into the prepared baking pan.
3. Drop apricot preserves by spoonfuls evenly over the coffee cake batter. Sprinkle with a mixture of the brown sugar and 1/2 teaspoon cinnamon.
4. Bake for 18 to 22 minutes or until a wooden pick inserted in the center comes out clean. Serve warm.

Approx Per Serving: Cal 198; Prot 4 g; Carbo 34 g; T Fat 5 g; 24% Calories from Fat; Chol 1 mg; Fiber <1 g; Sod 345 mg

Tip: *It is good to double this recipe in order to have a piece or two left over for a yummy snack.*

LIST YOUR ASSETS OF PERSONALITY AND TALENT. DON'T DWELL ON WHAT YOU MAY HAVE LOST OR HOW YOU ARE LIMITED. YOU WILL BEGIN TO FEEL BETTER INSTANTLY!

—Norman Vincent Peale

THE CREOLE CONNECTION

DILLY TOMATO SOUP

SHRIMP PONTCHARTRAIN

FLUFFY RICE

MANDARIN ORANGE SALAD

CLOVERLEAF ROLLS

SERVES 6

DESSERT SUGGESTION:

Cherries Jubilee (page 142)

WINE SUGGESTION:

A rich Pinot Noir with some spice to it is excellent with the shrimp and salad, adding a nice balance.

EN CONCERT SEQUENCE:

Prepare as much as possible ahead—the soup, rice and toast the almonds. Fix the Shrimp Pontchartrain in the afternoon and prepare salad but do not mix together until time to serve.

GROCERY LIST:

Groceries

- 6 cups tomato juice
- 1 bottle Tabasco sauce
- White pepper *
- 1 small jar dill pickles *
- Lemon juice *
- 8 ounces reduced-fat sour cream
- 1 jar prepared horseradish *
- 2 bunches green onions *
- 1 bunch fresh chives
- 1 package long grain white rice *
- 1½ pounds fresh medium shrimp
- ½ cup light cream
- 1 bunch fresh parsley
- 6 fresh medium mushrooms
- ½ cup sliced almonds *
- 8 ounces reduced-fat butter *
- 3 fresh kiwifruit
- 1 dozen fresh dinner rolls
- 1 head red lettuce
- 1 head Bibb lettuce
- 1 can mandarin oranges
- Long matches
- Vermouth *
- Raspberry vinegar *
- Creole seasoning

Staples

- Sugar, salt, pepper, garlic powder and cayenne
- Worcestershire sauce
- Chicken bouillon cubes
- Flour
- Olive oil
- Confectioners' sugar
- Mustard and poppy seeds

*Note: Staples are items that are usually found in the pantry—look before ordering. An * denotes items that could be considered staples for some families.*

Dilly Tomato Soup

6 cups tomato juice
1/4 cup sugar
1/2 teaspoon salt
1 teaspoon garlic powder
2 tablespoons Worcestershire sauce
1/4 teaspoon Tabasco sauce
1/2 cup each dill pickle juice and lemon juice
1/2 cup low-fat sour cream
1 teaspoon prepared horseradish
1/4 cup chopped chives

Microwave Method:

1. Combine the tomato juice, sugar, salt, garlic powder, Worcestershire sauce, Tabasco sauce, pickle juice and lemon juice in a microwave-safe 2-quart bowl.
2. Microwave on High (100%) until the mixture boils; stir. Microwave on Medium-High (70%) for 6 to 8 minutes, stirring once.
3. Mix the sour cream and horseradish in a small bowl.
4. Serve the soup immediately or chill the soup and sauce, covered, in the refrigerator for 8 to 12 hours. Microwave on High (100%) for 3 to 4 minutes, stir and cover. Microwave for 2 minutes longer just before serving.
5. Spoon the soup into serving bowls and top with a dollop of the horseradish sauce. Sprinkle with the chives.

Conventional Method:

1. Combine the tomato juice, sugar, salt, garlic powder, Worcestershire sauce, Tabasco sauce, pickle juice and lemon juice in a 2-quart saucepan with a lid. Cook, covered, until heated through and flavors blend.
2. Mix the sour cream and horseradish in a small bowl.
3. Serve the soup immediately or spoon into a bowl and chill the soup and sauce, covered, in the refrigerator for 8 to 12 hours; do not store in the saucepan.
4. Reheat the soup at serving time. Spoon into serving bowls and top with a dollop of the horseradish sauce. Sprinkle with the chives.

Approx Per Serving: Cal 110; Prot 3 g; Carbo 23 g; T Fat 2 g; 14% Calories from Fat; Chol 7 mg; Fiber 1 g; Sod 1172 mg

The body must be nourished, physically, emotionally and spiritually. We're spiritually starved in this culture—not underfed but undernourished.

—Carol Hornig

THE BODY IS A SACRED GARMENT. IT'S YOUR FIRST AND LAST GARMENT; IT IS WHAT YOU ENTER LIFE IN AND WHAT YOU DEPART LIFE WITH, AND IT SHOULD BE TREATED WITH HONOR.

—Martha Graham

SHRIMP PONTCHARTRAIN

This traditional dish can be found in several excellent restaurants in New Orleans. This is our favorite version—not too spicy or rich, just right. Preparing it in advance gets a lot of the cleanup out of the way and takes the pressure off, so you can enjoy your guests.

1 1/2 pounds fresh medium shrimp, rinsed, peeled, deveined
1 teaspoon Creole seasoning
1/2 cup reduced-fat butter
1 cup chopped green onions with tops
6 medium mushrooms, sliced
1/4 cup flour
1/2 cup light cream
1/4 cup vermouth
1/2 teaspoon salt
1/4 teaspoon white pepper
1/4 teaspoon cayenne
Fluffy Rice (page 103)

MICROWAVE METHOD:

1. Place the shrimp in a 1 1/2-quart microwave-safe dish and sprinkle with the Creole seasoning. Microwave, covered, on High (100%) for 5 minutes, stirring once. Drain, reserving half the liquid. Cover and set aside.
2. Microwave the butter on High (100%) in a microwave-safe dish for 1 minute or until melted. Add the green onions and mushrooms. Microwave on High (100%) for 3 to 4 minutes.
3. Stir in the flour. Add the reserved shrimp liquid, cream, vermouth, salt, white pepper and cayenne gradually, stirring constantly. Drain the shrimp again and add to the dish.
4. Microwave on Medium-High (70%) for 6 to 7 minutes, stirring twice. Serve over the Fluffy Rice. Garnish with fresh parsley and sliced fresh kiwifruit.

CONVENTIONAL METHOD:

1. Bring enough water to cover the shrimp to a boil in a 1 1/2-quart saucepan. Add the shrimp and return to a boil. Boil for 5 minutes or until the shrimp are pink. Drain, reserving 1/2 cup liquid.
2. Melt the butter in a saucepan. Add the green onions and mushrooms and sauté over medium heat until tender.

3. Reduce the heat and stir in the flour with a fork. Add the reserved shrimp liquid and remaining ingredients gradually, stirring constantly. Drain the shrimp again and add to the saucepan.
4. Cook over medium heat for 10 to 12 minutes, stirring occasionally. Serve over Fluffy Rice.

Approx Per Serving: Cal 235; Prot 16 g; Carbo 7 g; T Fat 14 g; 55% Calories from Fat; Chol 183 mg; Fiber 1 g; Sod 764 mg
Nutritional information does not include Fluffy Rice.

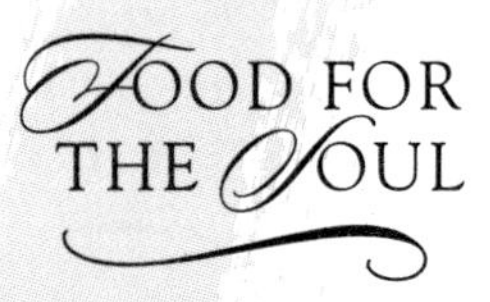

SOUL IS OUR APPETITE, DRIVING US TO EAT FROM THE BANQUET OF LIFE. PEOPLE FILLED WITH THE HUNGER OF SOUL TAKE FOOD FROM EVERY DISH BEFORE THEM, WHETHER IT BE SWEET OR BITTER.

—Matthew Fox, Ph.D.

FLUFFY RICE

Using the microwave method for this dish does not save any time, but the big advantage is that the rice does not stick to the pan and can be stored in the refrigerator in the same dish in which it is cooked. Either way works well. It's your choice.

2 1/2 cups hot water
1 cube chicken bouillon
1 1/2 cups uncooked long grain white rice
1/4 to 1/2 teaspoon pepper
Salt to taste

MICROWAVE METHOD:

1. Combine the hot water, bouillon, rice and pepper in a 2-quart microwave-safe dish and mix well. Microwave, covered, on High (100%) for 5 minutes; stir.
2. Microwave, covered, on Medium-High (70%) for 10 to 12 minutes. Microwave, uncovered, for 1 to 2 minutes longer. Salt to taste and let stand, covered, until serving time.

CONVENTIONAL METHOD:

1. Bring the water to a boil in a 2-quart saucepan. Stir in the bouillon until dissolved.
2. Add the rice, pepper and salt. Bring to a boil and stir. Reduce the heat and cover. Simmer for 15 to 20 minutes or until tender.

Approx Per Serving: Cal 171; Prot 3 g; Carbo 37 g; T Fat <1 g; 2% Calories from Fat; Chol <1 mg; Fiber 1 g; Sod 194 mg

A GREAT TEACHER NEVER STRIVES TO EXPLAIN HIS VISION—HE/SHE SIMPLY INVITES YOU TO STAND BESIDE HIM/HER AND SEE FOR YOURSELF.

—The Reverend R. Inman

MANDARIN ORANGE SALAD

The tart/sweet and juicy flavor of mandarin orange sections adds a tantalizing sparkle to the salad. The toasted almonds add a crunchy texture.

1/2 cup sliced almonds
2 tablespoons olive oil
1/4 cup raspberry vinegar
2 teaspoons confectioners' sugar
1/2 teaspoon mustard
1 teaspoon poppy seeds
1 head red lettuce, rinsed, torn
1 head Bibb lettuce, rinsed, torn
1/2 (8-ounce) can mandarin oranges, drained

METHOD:

1. Place the almonds in a glass pie plate. Microwave on High for 3 to 5 minutes or until toasted, stirring once. Cool and store in a sealable plastic bag.
2. For the dressing, combine the olive oil, vinegar, confectioners' sugar, mustard and poppy seeds in a glass jar. Cover and shake to mix well. Chill until serving time.
3. Combine the lettuce, almonds and oranges in a bowl. Shake the dressing again and add to the salad; toss to coat well. Serve on salad plates.

Approx Per Serving: Cal 116; Prot 3 g; Carbo 8 g; T Fat 9 g; 64% Calories from Fat; Chol 0 mg; Fiber 2 g; Sod 12 mg

CRISPY CHICKEN

JIFFY PASTA SALAD

PINEAPPLE BAKED BEANS

RELISH PLATE

FRENCH BAGUETTE WITH SESAME SEEDS

SERVES 6

DESSERT SUGGESTION:

Chocolate Cake (page 136) or Lite and Luscious Brownies (page 137)

WINE SUGGESTION:

A light, fruity Merlot would be especially good with this menu, without overwhelming the flavors.

EN CONCERT SEQUENCE:

This is a great menu to make ahead. If you are doing the entire menu in advance, wrap the Crispy Chicken in paper towels and then foil so it does not get soggy. If preparing at the last minute, begin with the pasta salad, then the relish plate and Crispy Chicken, followed by the Pineapple Baked Beans.

GROCERY LIST:

Groceries

- 1 (3½-pound) chicken
- 1 quart skim milk *
- 1 (16-ounce) package shell macaroni
- 1 head fresh broccoli
- 2 bunches green onions
- 1 green bell pepper
- 1 red bell pepper
- Fresh garlic *
- 1 (32-ounce) can baked beans
- 1 (8-ounce) can crushed pineapple
- 1 pint cherry tomatoes
- 8 ounces fat-free cream cheese
- 1 (16-ounce) package precut carrots and celery sticks
- 2 small zucchini
- 1 small bottle white vinegar *
- 1 long sesame French baguette
- 1 small bottle wine vinegar

Staples

- 3 eggs
- Seasoned dry bread crumbs
- Sesame seeds
- Seasoning salt
- Brown sugar
- Extra-light olive oil
- Mustard
- Reduced-fat margarine
- Ice
- Wooden picks
- Salt, black pepper, cayenne

*Note: Staples are items that are usually found in the pantry—look before ordering. An * denotes items that could be considered staples for some families.*

NO QUALITY IS MORE ATTRACTIVE THAN POISE—THAT DEEP SENSE OF BEING AT EASE WITH YOURSELF AND THE WORLD.

—Salman Rushdie

Crispy Chicken

The secret of this recipe is that the egg white disguises the fact that the chicken is skinless. It is tender, juicy and crispy, even when prepared in the microwave, in a matter of minutes.

3 egg whites, lightly beaten
1/4 cup skim milk
1/2 cup seasoned dry bread crumbs
2 teaspoons brown sugar
1 teaspoon sesame seeds
1 tablespoon seasoning salt
1 (3- to 3 1/2-pound) chicken, cut up, skin removed

Microwave Method:

1. Whisk the egg whites and skim milk together in a shallow bowl. Mix the bread crumbs, brown sugar, sesame seeds and seasoning salt on waxed paper. Dip the chicken in the egg white mixture and coat with the bread crumbs.
2. Arrange prepared chicken in a shallow microwave-safe dish with the thicker portions toward the outer edge and the wings toward the center. Cover with vented plastic wrap.
3. Microwave on High (100%) for 18 to 20 minutes (6 minutes per pound) or until the chicken is fork tender and the juices run clear. Turn the chicken and microwave for 30 to 60 seconds longer if any pink remains.
4. Replace the plastic wrap with paper towels to absorb moisture and let stand for 10 minutes.

Conventional Method:

1. Preheat the oven to 400 degrees. Follow Microwave Method Step 1.
2. Place the chicken on a foil-lined baking sheet and bake for 45 to 60 minutes or until the chicken is fork tender, the juices run clear and no pink remains.

Approx Per Serving: Cal 246; Prot 32 g; Carbo 10 g; T Fat 8 g; 30% Calories from Fat; Chol 84 mg; Fiber 1 g; Sod 841 mg

Jiffy Pasta Salad

Pasta salads come in all colors and personalities. This one boasts lots of healthy vegetables and a deliciously light piquant flavor. Pasta salads are usually better the second day, so if possible, prepare this the day before.

2 tablespoons reduced-fat margarine
3 medium cloves of garlic, crushed
1 tablespoon extra-light olive oil
2 teaspoons wine vinegar
1 teaspoon prepared mustard or dry mustard
1/2 teaspoon salt
1/4 teaspoon pepper
1 cup chopped broccoli florets
1/2 cup chopped green onions
1/4 cup chopped green bell pepper
1/4 cup chopped red bell pepper
3 cups drained cooked shell macaroni, al dente

Method:

1. For the dressing, combine the margarine, garlic, olive oil, vinegar, mustard, salt and pepper in a 2-cup glass measure. Microwave on High (100%) for 1 1/2 to 2 minutes; stir. Use immediately or store, tightly covered, in the refrigerator.
2. For the salad, combine the broccoli, green onions and bell peppers in a microwave-safe 1-quart dish with a lid. Microwave, covered, on High (100%) for 2 to 3 minutes or until tender-crisp. Let stand, uncovered, until cool.
3. Combine the pasta, vegetables and dressing in a large salad bowl and toss to mix well. Serve immediately or chill, tightly covered, until serving time.

Approx Per Serving: Cal 152; Prot 4 g; Carbo 23 g; T Fat 5 g; 30% Calories from Fat; Chol 0 mg; Fiber 2 g; Sod 254 mg

Tip: *To chill quickly, place cooked pasta and vegetables in a colander. Submerge the colander in a large bowl of ice water; drain.*

Learn to get in touch with the silence within yourself and know that everything in this life has a purpose. Find some time each day for quiet, it will enrich your life and those you love.

—Helen Kubler-Ross

Pineapple Baked Beans

Baked beans are low in fat, high in fiber, satisfying and require virtually no preparation. Wrap the hot beans in foil and place in a brown paper bag made of nonrecycled paper for the picnic. They will stay hot for almost an hour. Don't forget the serving spoon.

1 (32-ounce) can baked beans
1 (8-ounce) can crushed pineapple
1 tablespoon mustard
2 teaspoons brown sugar

Method:

1. Combine the beans, pineapple, mustard and brown sugar in a 2-quart microwave-safe dish or 2-quart saucepan and mix well.
2. Cover and microwave on High (100%) for 4 to 5 minutes or cook on the stove top until heated through; stir to mix well.

Approx Per Serving: Cal 178; Prot 8 g; Carbo 40 g; T Fat 1 g; 4% Calories from Fat; Chol 0 mg; Fiber 8 g; Sod 634 mg

To be happy at home is the ultimate result of all ambition.

—Samuel Johnson

In spite of the cost of living, it's still popular!

—Kathleen Norris

Relish Plate

To save time, buy the precut carrot and celery sticks. Just add a little dip and a few more vegetables and you're ready to go. Pair this plate with a nice French baguette with sesame seeds, and you've got your picnic!

1 (16-ounce) package precut carrot and celery sticks
2 small zucchini, cut into sticks
8 ounces fat-free cream cheese, whipped
1 bunch green onions, minced
1/4 teaspoon cayenne
1 pint cherry tomatoes

1. Place the carrots, celery and zucchini in ice water to crisp while you prepare the dip.
2. For the dip, mix the cream cheese, green onions and cayenne in a small bowl with a lid. Chill, covered, until serving time.
3. Place the dip in the center of a serving plate. Arrange the vegetable sticks and cherry tomatoes around the dip. Serve with decorated wooden picks.

Approx Per Serving: Cal 77; Prot 8 g; Carbo 12 g; T Fat <1 g; 3% Calories from Fat; Chol 3 mg; Fiber 3 g; Sod 237 mg

TOMATO CHUTNEY CHICKEN

QUICK TUBBY FRIES

CORN ON THE COB

GARLIC BREADSTICKS

SERVES 4

DESSERT SUGGESTION:

Angel Food Cake with Raspberry Purée (page 133)

WINE SUGGESTION:

A rich Zinfandel with a warm peppery finish will go particularly well with the chutney and complement this menu.

EN CONCERT SEQUENCE:

If possible, prepare the tomato chutney in advance to achieve the maximum blend of the seasonings. The day you prepare this menu, husk the corn according to the directions and set aside. Then micro-cook the potatoes and heat the barbecue. Once the barbecue is ready, grill the potatoes, followed by the chicken, and finally add the corn.

GROCERY LIST:

Groceries

- 2 (3½- to 4-pound) chickens
- 1 large red onion
- 4 medium tomatoes
- 4 medium baking potatoes
- 6 ears of corn
- 1 jar Paul Prudhomme's Magic Seasoning
- 1 package soft breadsticks

Staples

- Extra-virgin olive oil
- Curry powder
- Fresh or dry basil
- Sugar
- Red wine vinegar
- Seasoned salt
- Butter substitute
- Parsley flakes
- Salt and pepper
- Nonstick vegetable cooking spray
- Garlic powder
- Cornstarch

Note: Staples are items that are usually found in the pantry—look before ordering.

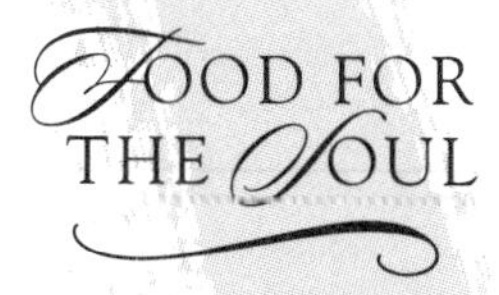

REMEMBER NOTHING IS DEADER THAN YESTERDAY. LEARN FROM YESTERDAY, AND GO ON. INSTEAD CAPITALIZE ON THE POSITIVES IN YOUR LIFE. THIS WILL OPEN YOUR MIND TO CREATIVE THOUGHTS AND NEW SOLUTIONS.

—Norman Vincent Peale

TOMATO CHUTNEY CHICKEN

The tomato chutney adds a new taste treat to traditional barbecued chicken, and was inspired by James Peterson's book Classical and Contemporary Sauce Making. *This en concert recipe assures delicious results in record time, with virtually none of the carcinogens associated with outdoor grilling.*

2 (3½- to 4-pound) chickens, split into halves, skin removed
1 large red onion, finely chopped
3 tablespoons extra-virgin olive oil
1½ tablespoons curry powder
1 teaspoon dry basil, or 1 tablespoon chopped fresh sweet basil
4 medium tomatoes, peeled, seeded, chopped
1½ tablespoons sugar
½ cup red wine vinegar
Salt to taste
½ teaspoon coarsely ground pepper

EN CONCERT METHOD (MICROWAVE AND GRILL):

1. Heat the grill. Place 2 chicken halves breast side down in a 7x11-inch microwave-safe dish; cover with vented plastic wrap. Microwave on High (100%) for 3 to 4 minutes per pound. Repeat with the remaining chicken.
2. Place the chicken on foil on the heated grill. Grill, covered, over medium coals for 15 to 20 minutes or until cooked through.
3. For the tomato chutney, combine the onion and olive oil in a 4-cup glass measure. Microwave on High (100%) for 3 to 4 minutes or until the onion is tender. Stir in the curry powder and basil.
4. Add the tomatoes, sugar and vinegar. Microwave for 6 to 8 minutes or until of the desired consistency. Season with salt and pepper.
5. Serve warm with the grilled chicken. Or may make ahead and store, covered, in the refrigerator to blend the flavors. Microwave on High (100%) for 2 to 4 minutes to reheat at serving time, stirring once.

The tomato chutney may also be prepared using the stovetop. You may substitute one 16-ounce can of drained and chopped tomatoes for the fresh tomatoes, adding them during the last 4 minutes of cooking time.

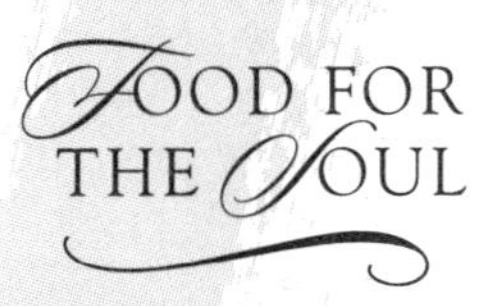

CONVENTIONAL METHOD:

1. Sauté the onion in the olive oil in a 2-quart saucepan over medium heat for 20 minutes, stirring every minute; do not brown. Add the curry powder and basil. Cook for 30 seconds or until the curry powder releases its aroma, stirring constantly.
2. Add the tomatoes, sugar and vinegar. Cook for 5 minutes or until thickened, stirring constantly. Spoon into a serving bowl and let stand until cool. Season with salt and pepper. Serve or store as above.

Approx Per Serving: Cal 793; Prot 97 g; Carbo 15 g; T Fat 36 g; 42% Calories from Fat; Chol 287 mg; Fiber 3 g; Sod 300 mg

INFINITE RICHES ARE ALL AROUND YOU IF YOU OPEN YOUR MENTAL EYES AND BEHOLD THE TREASURE HOUSE OF INFINITY WITHIN YOU. THERE IS A GOLD MINE WITHIN YOU FROM WHICH YOU CAN EXTRACT EVERYTHING YOU NEED TO LIVE LIFE GLORIOUSLY, JOYOUSLY AND ABUNDANTLY.

—Joseph Murphy

CORN ON THE COB

When we find sweet tender corn in the market, we know summer has arrived. This simple method of preparation is delightfully delicious and so easy!

6 ears of fresh corn with husks
2 tablespoons butter substitute
Salt and pepper to taste

EN CONCERT METHOD (MICROWAVE AND GRILL):

1. Preheat the grill. Remove the outer husks of the corn, leaving the inner layer. Mix the butter substitute, salt and pepper on waxed paper.
2. Place the corn on a rack in a shallow microwave-safe dish, alternating ends and leaving space between. Microwave on High (100%) for 1½ to 2 minutes per ear.
3. Place on the heated grill. Grill for 2 to 4 minutes or until tender, turning once. Remove the husks and roll the corn in the seasoning mixture. Wrap in foil to keep warm until serving time.

Approx Per Serving: Cal 125; Prot 4 g; Carbo 28 g; T Fat 2 g; 10% Calories from Fat; Chol <1 mg; Fiber 4 g; Sod 50 mg

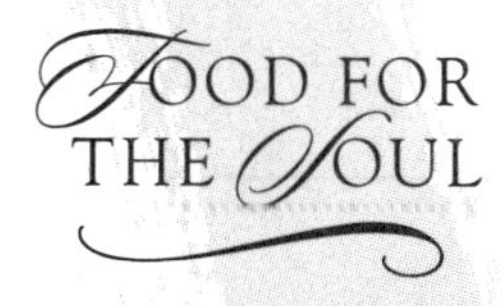

Quick Tubby Fries

A great way to enjoy the crispness of fried potatoes with none of the fat! Team your conventional oven or grill with the microwave oven to create these delicious "fakes" in less than 20 minutes. Experiment with your own favorite seasoning to personalize your Tubby Fries.

2 teaspoons butter substitute
2 teaspoons seasoned salt
1/2 teaspoon coarsely ground pepper
2 teaspoons parsley flakes
1/2 teaspoon Paul Prudhomme's Magic Seasoning
4 medium baking potatoes

En Concert Method (Microwave and Conventional):

1. Preheat the oven or the grill to 425 degrees. Mix the butter substitute, seasoned salt, pepper, parsley flakes and Magic Seasoning in a small dish.
2. Rinse the potatoes and pierce with a long-tined fork. Place on a rack in a microwave-safe dish, leaving a small space between each potato. Microwave on High (100%) for 6 minutes or until firm but not hard.
3. Cut the potatoes into halves and then into halves again to make 8 slices for each potato. Arrange on a large piece of foil or in a foil dish sprayed with nonstick vegetable cooking spray, leaving space between. Sprinkle with the seasoning mixture.
4. Bake or grill for 10 to 15 minutes or until crisp, turning several times to brown evenly. Serve immediately.

Conventional Method:

1. Preheat the oven and prepare the seasoning mix as in the En Concert Method Step 1. Cut the potatoes into halves and then into halves again to make 8 slices for each potato.
2. Arrange on a baking sheet sprayed with nonstick vegetable cooking spray, leaving space between. Sprinkle with the seasoning mixture.
3. Bake for 35 to 40 minutes or until crisp, turning several times to brown evenly.

Approx Per Serving: Cal 120; Prot 3 g; Carbo 28 g; T Fat <1 g; 1% Calories from Fat; Chol <1 mg; Fiber 2 g; Sod 476 mg

FAR AWAY THERE IN THE SUNSHINE ARE MY HIGHEST ASPIRATIONS. I MAY NOT REACH THEM, BUT I CAN LOOK UP AND SEE THEIR BEAUTY, BELIEVE IN THEM AND TRY TO FOLLOW WHERE THEY LEAD.

—Louisa May Alcott

Garlic Breadsticks

Choose your favorite prepared breadsticks and make them even more delicious with this nonfat trick.

4 soft breadsticks
1/4 cup Garlic Sauce (below)

Method:

1. Preheat the oven to 425 degrees.
2. Brush the breadsticks with the Garlic Sauce. Place on a baking sheet or foil sheet. Bake for 5 to 8 minutes or until heated through.

Approx Per Serving: Cal 46; Prot 1 g; Carbo 8 g; T Fat 1 g; 19% Calories from Fat; Chol <1 mg; Fiber <1 g; Sod 78 mg

It is not fair to ask of others what you are not willing to do yourself.

—*Eleanor Roosevelt*

Garlic Sauce

This "buttery" garlic sauce can be stored, covered, in the refrigerator for up to 3 days and can also be used as a flavor lift for vegetable dishes.

2 teaspoons cornstarch
1 cup water
1/4 cup butter substitute
1 teaspoon garlic powder

Microwave Method:

1. Blend the cornstarch with the water in a 2-cup glass measure.
2. Microwave on High (100%) for 1 1/4 to 2 minutes or until bubbly, stirring once. Stir in the butter substitute and garlic powder.

Yields 20 (1-tablespoon) servings

Approx Per Serving: Cal 5; Prot <1 g; Carbo 1 g; T Fat <1 g; 2% Calories from Fat; Chol <1 mg; Fiber <1 g; Sod 12 mg

ORANGE-GLAZED CORNISH GAME HENS

PARSLIED RED POTATOES

FRESH ASPARAGUS BUNDLES

SPINACH SALAD

SERVES 4

DESSERT SUGGESTION:

Chocolate Angel Meringues (page 130)

WINE SUGGESTION:

An off-dry and very fruity wine will be a winner with this menu. Select a Riesling, Gewürztraminer, or off-dry Chardonnay.

GROCERY LIST:

Groceries

2 Cornish game hens
1 (11-ounce) can mandarin oranges
1 (12-ounce) package fresh spinach
1 pint cherry tomatoes
1 red onion
3 fresh mushrooms
1 (4-ounce) package dried apricots
1 bottle nonfat raspberry salad dressing
5 red potatoes
1 pound fresh asparagus
Dark molasses *

Staples

Browning sauce
Brown sugar
Cornstarch
Cinnamon
Parsley flakes or fresh parsley
Basil
Reduced-fat margarine
Salt and pepper
Lemon juice
Nonstick vegetable cooking spray

*Note: Staples are items that are usually found in the pantry—look before ordering. An * denotes items that could be considered staples for some families.*

Orange-Glazed Cornish Game Hens

These succulent hens are quick to prepare, very versatile, and ready in just 12 to 13 minutes in the microwave. The sauce adds a delicate flavor and sparkling glaze.

2 Cornish game hens
1 tablespoon each browning sauce (i.e., Kitchen Bouquet) and water
1 (11-ounce) can mandarin oranges
2 teaspoons cornstarch
1 teaspoon each dark molasses and brown sugar
Cinnamon to taste

Microwave Method:

1. Rinse the game hens inside and out, discarding the skin and fat; pat dry. Brush with a mixture of the browning sauce and water.
2. Place breast side down in a 2-quart microwave-safe dish, leaving space between. Cover with vented plastic wrap.
3. Microwave on High (100%) for 6 minutes. Turn breast side up and cover. Microwave for 6 1/2 to 7 minutes or until the juice runs clear and the leg moves easily. Let stand, covered, for 5 minutes.
4. For the orange sauce, drain the oranges, reserving the juice and half the oranges; store the remaining oranges for another use. Blend the cornstarch, molasses, brown sugar and cinnamon in a 2-cup glass measure. Stir in the reserved orange juice.
5. Microwave on High (100%) for 1 1/2 minutes or until thickened, stirring after 30 seconds. Stir in reserved oranges. Serve over hens.

Conventional Method:

1. Preheat oven to 350 degrees. Follow Microwave Method Step 1.
2. Place the hens in a baking dish sprayed with nonstick vegetable cooking spray, leaving space between. Bake, covered with foil, for 40 minutes or until the juice runs clear and the leg moves easily.
3. Follow Microwave Method Step 4, blending the mixture in a 1-quart saucepan. Cook over medium-high heat until thickened. Stir in the reserved oranges. Serve over the hens.

Approx Per Serving: Cal 275; Prot 36 g; Carbo 9 g; T Fat 9 g; 31% Calories from Fat; Chol 110 mg; Fiber <1 g; Sod 397 mg
Nutritional information includes only 1/2 can mandarin oranges.

Nothing in the world can take the place of Persistence. Talent will not; nothing is more commonplace than unsuccessful men with talent. Genius will not; unrewarded genius is almost a proverb. Education alone will not; the world is full of educated derelicts. Persistence and Determination alone are omnipotent.

—Calvin Coolidge

THE FUTURE BELONGS TO THOSE WHO BELIEVE IN THE BEAUTY OF THEIR DREAMS.

—*Eleanor Roosevelt*

PARSLIED RED POTATOES

Potatoes kept sailors of old from contracting scurvy on long voyages. Today we can enjoy their delicious flavor and know they are good for us, too.

5 small red potatoes
1 tablespoon parsley flakes or chopped fresh parsley
1 teaspoon dried basil
1 tablespoon reduced-fat margarine
Salt and pepper to taste

MICROWAVE METHOD:

1. Rinse the potatoes and slice each lengthwise. Combine with the parsley, basil and margarine in a 2-quart microwave-safe dish with a lid.
2. Microwave on High (100%) for 6 to 7 minutes or until tender, stirring once. Season with salt and pepper. Let stand, covered, for 5 minutes. Potatoes will stay hot for 10 minutes. Microwave on Medium-High (70%) for 2 minutes to reheat if necessary.

CONVENTIONAL METHOD:

1. Slice the potatoes as in Step 1 in the Microwave Method. Bring 2 inches of water to a boil in a 2-quart saucepan. Add the potatoes.
2. Cook over medium heat for 20 minutes or until tender; drain most of the liquid. Add the remaining ingredients. Cook over low heat for 2 to 3 minutes, stirring gently to coat well. Cover until serving time.

Approx Per Serving: Cal 142; Prot 3 g; Carbo 29 g; T Fat 2 g; 12% Calories from Fat; Chol 0 mg; Fiber 3 g; Sod 43 mg

Fresh Asparagus Bundles

The first tender stalks of asparagus came from the volcanic slopes of Mount Vesuvius in Italy. According to Charles Lamb, they bring "gentle thoughts." So here's to gentle thoughts and delicious eating!

1 pound fresh asparagus
2 teaspoons reduced-fat margarine
1 teaspoon lemon juice

Microwave Method:

1. Snap off any tough ends from the asparagus stalks; rinse the asparagus in cold water.
2. Arrange in a microwave-safe dish with the tips toward the center. Spread with a mixture of the margarine and lemon juice.
3. Microwave, covered with vented plastic wrap, on High (100%) for 6 to 7 minutes or until tender-crisp, stirring gently once.

Conventional Method:

1. Follow Step 1 in the Microwave Method.
2. Combine the asparagus with 1/4 cup water in a large skillet sprayed with nonstick vegetable cooking spray. Add the margarine and lemon juice.
3. Cook over medium-high heat for 6 to 8 minutes or until tender-crisp.

Approx Per Serving: Cal 36; Prot 3 g; Carbo 5 g; T Fat 1 g; 29% Calories from Fat; Chol 0 mg; Fiber 2 g; Sod 24 mg

Consider today as a new beginning. Remind yourself that all your yesterdays ended last night. Forget your past and believe in your future.

—Norman Vincent Peale

It is very important to learn to like yourself. Look in the mirror at night before retiring and tell yourself you did a good job today. If the day didn't go as well as it might have tell yourself tomorrow I will do this better—never say "if only I had." You will do better tomorrow!

—*Norman Vincent Peale*

Spinach Salad

The crispy spinach in this salad gives color, texture, and flavor to the menu.

1 (12-ounce) package leaf spinach, torn
1 pint cherry tomatoes, cut into halves
1 small red onion, thinly sliced
3 fresh mushrooms, thinly sliced
4 dried apricots, chopped
1/4 cup nonfat raspberry salad dressing

Method:

1. Combine the spinach, tomatoes, onion, mushrooms and dried apricots in a salad bowl.
2. Add the raspberry salad dressing and toss to coat well.

Approx Per Serving: Cal 93; Prot 4 g; Carbo 20 g; T Fat 1 g; 6% Calories from Fat; Chol 0 mg; Fiber 4 g; Sod 76 mg

POTTED TURKEY

LIGHT-SIDE POTATO SALAD

ICED VEGETABLE PLATE

POPPY SEED BUNS

SERVES 6

DESSERT SUGGESTION:

Watermelon and/or Marble Cake on the Light Side (Page 135)

WINE SUGGESTION:

Either white or red wine can be served with this menu. For a white wine, select a nice Riesling or Gewürztraminer; for red, try a Gamay Beaujolais. Both wines have a fruity taste that will bring out the richness of the turkey and its marinade.

EN CONCERT SEQUENCE:

Most of this menu can be prepared in advance. Prepare the potato salad, pack the vegetables in ice and place the turkey in the marinade on the day before, leaving nothing but cooking the turkey for the day of the supper.

GROCERY LIST:

Groceries

1 (5-pound) turkey breast
1 pint bourbon
3 pounds red potatoes
1 carton eggs *
1 carton egg substitute *
1 small jar sweet pickles *
1 bunch green onions
1 bottle tarragon vinegar *
1 bunch celery
3 tomatoes
3 zucchini
1 (8-ounce) package precut cauliflower and broccoli
1 (8-ounce) package precut carrot and celery sticks
Tiny crabapples
Grapes
1 (12-count) package poppy seed buns

Staples

Extra-virgin olive oil
Soy sauce
Worcestershire sauce
Garlic powder
Salt and pepper
Lemon juice
Celery seeds
Prepared mustard
Nonstick vegetable cooking spray

*Note: Staples are items that are usually found in the pantry—look before ordering. An * denotes items that could be considered staples for some families.*

DON'T WASTE TIME ON POST-MORTEMS. START THINKING ABOUT WHAT TO DO NOW. AMAZING THINGS HAPPEN WHEN YOU THINK CONSTRUCTIVELY.

—Norman Vincent Peale

POTTED TURKEY

Serve this first as an elegant entrée and enjoy any leftovers in thin slices for sandwiches or as a tasty addition to a summer salad.

1/2 cup extra-virgin olive oil
1/2 cup bourbon
3 tablespoons soy sauce
2 teaspoons Worcestershire sauce
2 teaspoons garlic powder
Pepper to taste
1 (5-pound) turkey breast

EN CONCERT METHOD (MICROWAVE AND GRILL):

1. For the marinade, combine the olive oil, bourbon, soy sauce, Worcestershire sauce, garlic powder and pepper in a 2-cup glass measure.
2. Rinse the turkey and pat dry; split into halves, and remove skin. Pierce several times with a long-tined fork. Combine with the marinade in a double layer of large food storage bags; tie up end of the bags.
3. Marinate in the refrigerator for 6 hours or longer, turning once or twice; drain.
4. Place the turkey skin side down in a 3-quart microwave-safe dish. Cover with vented plastic wrap. Microwave on High (100%) for 4 minutes per pound, turning skin side up after 10 minutes.
5. Preheat the grill. Place the turkey on the grill rack. Grill for 10 minutes per pound or until the juices run clear, turning once or twice. Let stand, covered with foil, for 10 minutes. Cut diagonally into slices. Garnish with tiny crabapples and frosted grapes.

Approx Per Serving: Cal 292; Prot 32 g; Carbo <1 g; T Fat 15 g; 48% Calories from Fat; Chol 81 mg; Fiber 0 g; Sod 339 mg
Nutritional information based on 15 servings.

Tip: *An easy way to frost grapes is to dip them in water and then into sugar, place on paper towel and let dry.*

Light-Side Potato Salad

Summer wouldn't be summer without a tasty old-fashioned potato salad, but it can be loaded with fat. This recipe retains the flavor and is still on the light side, and takes minutes to prepare.

1/4 cup extra-virgin olive oil
1 tablespoon tarragon vinegar
1 teaspoon each prepared mustard and lemon juice
1/2 teaspoon celery seeds
1/4 teaspoon pepper
3 pounds red potatoes, cut into 1-inch pieces
1 egg
1/2 cup egg substitute, or the equivalent of 2 eggs
5 green onions, chopped
4 sweet pickles, finely chopped
1/4 cup sweet pickle juice
2 ribs celery, chopped
Salt and pepper to taste

En Concert Method (Microwave and Conventional):

1. For the salad dressing, combine the olive oil, vinegar, mustard, lemon juice, celery seeds and 1/4 teaspoon pepper in a food processor or blender container and process until smooth. Store in a covered jar in the refrigerator until time to use.
2. Place the potatoes in a 3-quart microwave-safe dish; cover with lid. Microwave on High (100%) for 5 to 6 minutes per pound or until tender. Cool to room temperature.
3. Boil the egg in water to cover in a saucepan until cooked through; drain and chop.
4. Place the egg substitute in a shallow microwave-safe dish covered with vented plastic wrap. Microwave on High (100%) for 1 1/2 to 2 minutes, stirring once. Let stand, covered, for 3 minutes. Cut into small pieces. Mix with the potatoes, boiled egg, green onions, pickles, pickle juice and celery in a large salad bowl.
5. Add the dressing, salt and pepper to taste; toss to mix. Chill, covered, until serving time.

Approx Per Serving: Cal 306; Prot 7 g; Carbo 47 g; T Fat 11 g; 31% Calories from Fat; Chol 36 mg; Fiber 3 g; Sod 353 mg

Tip: *May cook the egg substitute in a small skillet sprayed with nonstick vegetable cooking spray over medium heat until set if preferred.*

Settle one difficulty and you keep hundreds away.

—*Chinese Proverb*

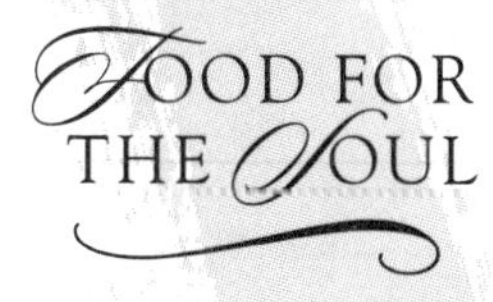

LIVE YOUR LIFE
AND FORGET
YOUR AGE!

—*Norman Vincent Peale*

ICED VEGETABLE PLATE

Substitute your favorite vegetables for the ones suggested here. Their crisp snap will be a delicious complement to the turkey and salad.

3 zucchini
1 (8-ounce) package precut cauliflower and broccoli
1 (8-ounce) package precut carrot and celery sticks
3 tomatoes

METHOD:

1. Cut each zucchini lengthwise into 8 slices. Soak the zucchini, cauliflower, broccoli, carrot sticks and celery sticks in ice water in a bowl for 1 hour.
2. Bring water to a boil in a 2-quart saucepan. Add the tomatoes. Boil for 30 seconds. Remove the tomatoes with a long-tined fork and remove the skins. Chill in ice water.
3. Drain the tomatoes and cut into wedges. Drain the remaining vegetables. Arrange all of the chilled vegetables on a plate. Chill, covered with plastic wrap, until serving time.

Approx Per Serving: Cal 55; Prot 3 g; Carbo 11 g; T Fat 1 g; 14% Calories from Fat; Chol 0 mg; Fiber 4 g; Sod 146 mg

Simply Scrumptious Supper

Pork Medallions with Cranberry Mustard Sauce

Garlic Mashed Potatoes

Ellie's Roasted Veggies

Stuffed Pear Salad

Serves 4

Dessert Suggestion:

Lite and Luscious Brownies (page 137)

Wine Suggestion:

Select your favorite Pinot Noir, Red Zinfandel, Sangiovese, Grenache, or any Beaujolais for this meal.

En Concert:

Begin with preparing the pork and the sauce. While the pork medallions are cooking, roast the veggies and make the mashed potatoes.

Grocery List:

Groceries

- 1½ pounds pork tenderloin
- 1 small package dried cranberries or tart cherries
- 1 (10-ounce) jar cranberry sauce
- 1 jar Dijon mustard
- Fat-free raspberry salad dressing
- 8 ounces fat-free sour cream
- 1 package instant potato flakes
- 1 zucchini
- 1 red bell pepper
- 1 yellow bell pepper
- 1 medium eggplant
- 1 medium red onion
- 1 pattypan squash
- 1 large tomato
- 1 bottle balsamic vinaigrette
- 1 (32-ounce) can pear halves
- 1 (4-ounce) container cranberry-orange relish
- Mint leaves *

Staples

- Nonstick vegetable cooking spray
- Cornstarch
- Strawberry jelly
- Skim milk
- Reduced-fat margarine
- Garlic powder or fresh garlic (several cloves)
- Olive oil
- Salt and pepper

*Note: Staples are items that are usually found in the pantry—look before ordering. An * denotes items that could be considered staples for some families.*

ENJOY BEING ALIVE. I LIKE LIVING, I HAVE SOMETIMES BEEN WILDLY, DESPAIRINGLY, ACUTELY MISERABLE, RACKED WITH SORROW, BUT THROUGH IT ALL I STILL KNOW QUITE CERTAINLY THAT JUST TO BE ALIVE IS A GRAND THING.

—*Agatha Christie*

PORK MEDALLIONS WITH CRANBERRY MUSTARD SAUCE

To prepare the cranberry mustard called for in this recipe, just mix one 10-ounce jar of 100% fruit cranberry sauce with 1 tablespoon of Dijon mustard. Store it in a covered jar in the refrigerator to serve on pork, white fish, and chicken.

1/3 cup dried cranberries or tart cherries
1/4 cup water
1 tablespoon cranberry mustard (above)
1/3 cup fat-free raspberry salad dressing
2 tablespoons strawberry jelly
1 1/2 pounds pork tenderloin
2 teaspoons cornstarch
3 tablespoons water
Salt and pepper to taste

EN CONCERT METHOD (MICROWAVE AND CONVENTIONAL):

1. For the sauce, combine the cranberries and 1/4 cup water in a 2-cup glass measure. Microwave on High (100%) for 1 1/2 minutes. Add the cranberry mustard, salad dressing and jelly and mix well.
2. Cut the pork diagonally into 1/2-inch slices. Heat a skillet sprayed with nonstick vegetable cooking spray until hot. Add the pork and cook until brown on both sides.
3. Add the sauce to the skillet. Cook, covered, over medium heat for 5 minutes.
4. Blend the cornstarch with 3 tablespoons water in a cup. Push the pork medallions to 1 side in the skillet and stir in the cornstarch mixture. Cook over low heat for 2 to 3 minutes or until slightly thickened, stirring constantly. Season with salt and pepper.

Approx Per Serving: Cal 305; Prot 36 g; Carbo 23 g; T Fat 6 g; 19% Calories from Fat; Chol 101 mg; Fiber 1 g; Sod 81 mg

Tip: *This recipe doubles beautifully to serve eight.*

Garlic Mashed Potatoes

Once thought to be only for the holidays or Sunday dinner, garlic mashed potatoes are ready in a flash with this method.

1¹/₃ cups skim milk
1 tablespoon reduced-fat margarine
1¹/₃ cups instant potato flakes
3 tablespoons fat-free sour cream
¹/₂ teaspoon garlic powder, or 1 small clove of garlic, crushed
Salt and pepper to taste

Microwave Method:

1. Combine the milk and margarine in a 1¹/₂-quart microwave-safe dish. Microwave on High (100%) for 3 minutes or until boiling.
2. Stir in the potato flakes, sour cream, garlic powder, salt and pepper. Whip until fluffy. Keep warm, covered, until serving time.

Conventional Method:

1. Bring the skim milk and margarine to a boil in a saucepan.
2. Follow Microwave Method Step 2.

Approx Per Serving: Cal 97; Prot 4 g; Carbo 15 g; T Fat 2 g; 18% Calories from Fat; Chol 1 mg; Fiber 0 g; Sod 93 mg

TAKE A MINUTE AND FIND A SONG THROUGH YOUR FAVORITE MUSIC; LISTEN, HUM ALONG, TAKE A FEW MOMENTS TO SUBMERGE YOURSELF... ITS MESSAGE WILL SOOTHE YOU... IMPROVING YOUR PERSPECTIVE.

INTUITION IS A SPIRITUAL FACULTY, AND DOES NOT EXPLAIN, BUT SIMPLY POINTS THE WAY.

—Florence Scovel Shinn

ELLIE'S ROASTED VEGGIES

These roasted veggies are succulently delicious and a snap to do. Cut them up in advance and place in a sealable plastic bag until ready to pop in the oven. Leftovers make a delightful lunch with a piece of crusty bread and some fruit.

2 tablespoons extra-virgin olive oil
2 to 3 cloves of garlic, crushed
1 zucchini, cut into 1/2-inch-round pieces
1 red bell pepper, sliced into 1/4-inch strips
1 yellow bell pepper, sliced into 1/4-inch strips
1 medium eggplant, peeled, sliced into 1/2x2-inch strips
1 medium red onion, thickly sliced
2 cups sliced yellow and green pattypan squash
1 large tomato, cut into quarters
1/4 cup fat-free balsamic vinaigrette

METHOD:

1. Preheat oven to 425 degrees.
2. Combine olive oil and garlic in a small dish.
3. Line a baking sheet with foil. Spray with nonstick vegetable cooking spray. Arrange the vegetables on the prepared baking sheet. Brush vegetables with the olive oil mixture. Bake for 15 minutes.
4. Pour the balsamic vinaigrette evenly over the vegetables and stir gently. Bake for 5 to 8 minutes longer or until the vegetables are tender. Place on a vegetable platter. Garnish with parsley.

Approx Per Serving: Cal 100; Prot 3 g; Carbo 14 g; T Fat 5 g; 41% Calories from Fat; Chol 0 mg; Fiber 4 g; Sod 89 mg

Stuffed Pear Salad

This salad, with its fresh sweet/tart flavor, can even masquerade as a dessert.

8 canned pear halves, chilled
1 (4-ounce) container cranberry-orange relish
Mint leaves (optional)

Method:

1. Arrange 2 pear halves on salad plates or in individual fruit dishes.
2. Spoon cranberry-orange relish into the center of each pear. Place 1 mint leaf under the edge of 1 pear half on each plate.

Approx Per Serving: Cal 163; Prot <1 g; Carbo 42 g; T Fat <1 g; 1% Calories from Fat; Chol 0 mg; Fiber 3 g; Sod 17 mg

Attitude is everything... keep it positive by being thankful for all the good in your life as you start each day.

Delicious Desserts

Chocolate Angel Meringues

Angel Food Cake with Peach Sauce

Angel Food Cake with Raspberry Purée

Angel Short Cake

Marble Cake on the Light Side

Chocolate Cake

Lite and Luscious Brownies

Mom's Apple Pie

Cinnamon Baked Apples

Blueberry-Peach Crisp

Blueberry Tapioca Pudding

Cherries Jubilee

Cranberry-Apple Crisp

Lemon Meringue Pie

Fresh Peach Melba

Raspberry-Blueberry Whip

Instant Strawberry Cake

Passionate Strawberries

Strawberry-Tapioca Swirl

Sweet Ambrosia

Fruit Kabobs with Chocolate Dip

Waikiki Sundaes

Light Chocolate Sauce in a Jiffy

MOST PEOPLE ARE AS HAPPY AS THEY MAKE UP THEIR MINDS TO BE. NINETY-EIGHT PERCENT OF HAPPINESS IS IN THE MIND.

—Abraham Lincoln

CHOCOLATE ANGEL MERINGUES

You'll love this cold, sweet confection, so easy and LOW IN FAT! A chocolate lover's fantasy and the answer to a delicious dessert. Indulge!

1/2 cup skim milk
1 envelope whipped topping mix
1/2 teaspoon vanilla extract
1 tablespoon baking cocoa
1 1/2 cups fresh chopped peaches (or raspberries, blueberries or a medley of the three)
Chocolate Sauce (page 131)

METHOD:

1. Combine the milk, whipped topping mix, vanilla and baking cocoa in a mixer bowl.
2. Beat at high speed until soft peaks form. Beat for 2 minutes longer or until light and fluffy.
3. Spoon onto a foil-lined baking sheet, shaping the mixture into 4-inch shells.
4. Place in the freezer. Freeze until firm.
5. Fill the center of each shell with the peaches. Drizzle with the Chocolate Sauce.

SERVES 5

Approx Per Serving: Cal 239; Prot 2 g; Carbo 46 g; T Fat 5 g; 18% Calories from Fat; Chol <1 mg; Fiber 3 g; Sod 81 mg

Chocolate Sauce

Chocolaty, velvety, and low in fat! The chocolate lover's answer to satisfying the sweet tooth without drowning in fat. For hot fudge sundaes, heat the sauce in the microwave on Medium-High (70%) for 20 to 30 seconds.

- 1/2 cup sugar
- 3 1/2 tablespoons baking cocoa
- 1 1/2 tablespoons cornstarch
- 1/8 teaspoon salt
- 1/2 cup water
- 2 teaspoons reduced-fat margarine or butter
- 1 teaspoon vanilla extract

Microwave Method:

1. Combine the sugar, baking cocoa, cornstarch and salt in a 2-cup glass measure. Stir in the water.
2. Microwave on High (100%) for 2 minutes, stirring twice. Add the margarine.
3. Microwave for 15 seconds longer. Add the vanilla, stirring until smooth. If the sauce is too thick, stir in a small amount of water.
4. Store in the refrigerator in a covered bowl.

Conventional Method:

1. Combine the sugar, baking cocoa, cornstarch and salt in a small saucepan. Stir in the water.
2. Cook over medium heat until the mixture begins to boil, stirring constantly.
3. Boil for 1 minute; remove from the heat.
4. Add the margarine and vanilla, stirring until smooth. If the sauce is too thick, stir in a small amount of water.
5. Store in the refrigerator in a covered bowl.

Serves 5

Approx Per Serving: Cal 103; Prot 1 g; Carbo 24 g; T Fat 1 g; 8% Calories from Fat; Chol 0 mg; Fiber 1 g; Sod 68 mg

Be an optimist! An optimist is a person who takes the cold water thrown on his idea, heats it with enthusiasm, makes steam, and pushes ahead!

—Anonymous

SAFETY IS THE MOST UNSAFE SPIRITUAL PATH YOU CAN TAKE. SAFETY KEEPS YOU NUMB AND DEAD. PEOPLE ARE CAUGHT BY SURPRISE WHEN IT IS TIME TO DIE. THEY HAVE ALLOWED THEMSELVES SO LITTLE.

—Stephen Levine

Angel Food Cake with Peach Sauce

Angel food cake is easily made with a good mix, or pick one up in the bakery section already made. Fresh peaches abound in the late summer months and add such a heavenly finalé. Be sure to pick ripe peaches that are slightly soft to the touch. Bon appétit!

2 teaspoons cornstarch
1/4 cup water
1 1/2 tablespoons sugar
3 to 4 ripe peaches, peeled, thinly sliced
1/4 teaspoon almond extract
1 angel food cake, sliced

Microwave Method:

1. Dissolve the cornstarch in the water in a 4-cup glass measure. Add the sugar and peaches, stirring to mix.
2. Microwave on High (100%) for 3 1/2 to 4 1/2 minutes or until the mixture comes to a boil, stirring twice.
3. Let stand to cool.
4. Spoon the peach sauce over individual cake slices and garnish with fresh raspberries or strawberries and sprigs of mint.

Conventional Method:

1. Dissolve the cornstarch in the water in a small saucepan. Add the sugar and peaches.
2. Cook over medium heat until the mixture begins to boil, stirring constantly. Reduce the heat to low. Cook for 1 to 2 minutes longer; cool.
3. Spoon the peach sauce over individual cake slices and garnish with fresh raspberries or strawberries and sprigs of mint.

Serves 10

Approx Per Serving: Cal 99; Prot 2 g; Carbo 23 g; T Fat <1 g; 2% Calories from Fat; Chol 0 mg; Fiber 1 g; Sod 212 mg

Tip: *Frozen sliced peaches are good too. If using frozen peaches, puncture the package with a fork to vent. Place on a paper plate. Microwave on Defrost (30%) for 3 to 4 minutes. Make the sauce following the instructions for fresh peaches, increasing the cornstarch to 1 tablespoon.*

Angel Food Cake with Raspberry Purée

Here is another luscious version of the versatile angel food cake. Add this elegant ruby-red sauce, and you'll have a satisfied sweet tooth! This sauce is also delicious served warm over frozen yogurt and fruit.

2 (10-ounce) packages frozen raspberries
2 tablespoons red raspberry jelly
1 envelope whipped topping mix
1 angel food cake, sliced

Microwave Method:

1. Pierce the raspberry packages with a fork to vent.
2. Microwave on High (100%) for 2 1/2 minutes to defrost the raspberries.
3. Combine with the jelly in a food processor or blender container. Process until puréed. Strain into a 4-cup glass measure.
4. Microwave on High (100%) for 5 minutes or until the mixture begins to boil. Microwave for 3 minutes longer; stir. Strain into a bowl. Chill, covered with plastic wrap.
5. Prepare the whipped topping using package directions, substituting skim milk for whole milk.
6. Spoon the raspberry sauce over individual slices of the cake. Serve with a dollop of whipped topping.

Conventional Method:

1. Place the raspberry packages in a large bowl of warm water. Let stand for 15 minutes to thaw.
2. Combine with the jelly in a food processor or blender container. Process until puréed. Strain into a 1-quart saucepan.
3. Bring to a boil. Boil for 3 minutes, stirring occasionally. Strain into a bowl. Chill, covered with plastic wrap.
4. Prepare topping and serve cake following Microwave Method Steps 5 and 6.

Serves 10

Approx Per Serving: Cal 168; Prot 3 g; Carbo 37 g; T Fat 1 g; 6% Calories from Fat; Chol <1 mg; Fiber 3 g; Sod 221 mg

It is good to remember that each day we live we never live again. Let's give it our best!

SOFTEN THE EDGE OF A HARD DAY OR DIFFICULT PERIOD BY ALLOWING YOURSELF A LITTLE SOMETHING THAT CAN MAKE YOU SMILE, FEEL LOVED OR JUST SATISFIED.

ANGEL SHORT CAKE

Calling all dessert lovers! For a satisfying end to your meal without guilt or extra pounds, try this fun and easy angel food cake variation.

1 pint fresh strawberries, or 1 (8-ounce) package frozen strawberries
1 tablespoon confectioners' sugar
1 angel food cake, sliced
Fat-free whipped topping

METHOD:

1. Rinse the strawberries and remove the stems. Cut the strawberries into slices and place in a bowl. Sprinkle with the confectioners' sugar. If using frozen strawberries, place on a paper plate and Microwave on High (100%) for 2 to 2½ minutes to defrost. Let stand for 5 to 10 minutes before spooning over the cake.
2. Top individual portions of the cake with the strawberries. Serve with the whipped topping. Garnish with fresh mint and edible flowers, such as pansies or geraniums.

SERVES 10

Approx Per Serving: Cal 85; Prot 2 g; Carbo 19 g; T Fat <1 g; 3% Calories from Fat; Chol 0 mg; Fiber 1 g; Sod 213 mg

Marble Cake on the Light Side

This is a great way to cut down on fat grams and never know it. If you are in a hurry to eat, sprinkle the warm cake with confectioners' sugar and serve with fat-free yogurt.

1 (2-layer) package marble cake mix
2 cups confectioners' sugar
3 tablespoons baking cocoa
1/4 cup skim milk
1 teaspoon vanilla extract

Method:

1. Prepare the cake mix using package directions, substituting egg substitute for whole eggs. Bake using package directions.
2. Combine the confectioners' sugar and baking cocoa in a bowl. Mix the milk and vanilla in a cup. Pour into the dry ingredients gradually, beating constantly with a wooden spoon until thick and creamy. May add 1/2 to 1 teaspoon milk to the frosting if needed for desired spreading consistency.
3. Spread the chocolate frosting over the cooled cake.

Serves 16

Approx Per Serving: Cal 250; Prot 3 g; Carbo 42 g; T Fat 8 g; 29% Calories from Fat; Chol <1 mg; Fiber 1 g; Sod 246 mg

To soothe your soul, try a hot bath using a fragrance you love. Sip a hot cup of tea snuggled in your favorite chair. Listen to soothing music and indulge with a piece of chocolate!

"MODERN CONDITIONS" ARE TREATED AS FIXED, THOUGH THE VERY WORD "MODERN" IMPLIES THAT THEY ARE FUGITIVE. "OLD IDEAS" ARE TREATED AS IMPOSSIBLE, THOUGH THEIR VERY ANTIQUITY OFTEN PROVES THEIR PERMANENCE.

—Samuel Johnson

CHOCOLATE CAKE

This delicious recipe is worth a little extra time. It's chocolaty (for us chocoholics!) and still low in fat and calories. Say, this low-fat eating is getting better all the time.

6 tablespoons reduced-fat margarine
1 cup sugar
1 cup skim milk
1 tablespoon white vinegar
1/2 teaspoon vanilla extract
1 1/4 cups flour
1/3 cup baking cocoa
1 teaspoon baking soda

METHOD:

1. Preheat oven to 350 degrees. Spray two 8-inch cake pans with nonstick vegetable cooking spray.
2. Place the reduced-fat margarine in a 1-quart glass measuring cup. Microwave on High (100%) for 20 to 30 seconds or until melted.
3. Stir in the sugar. Add the milk, vinegar and vanilla, stirring well.
4. Mix the flour, baking cocoa and baking soda together. Whisk into the sugar mixture. Pour into prepared cake pans.
5. Bake at 350 degrees for 20 minutes or until a wooden pick inserted near the center comes out clean.
6. Cool in the pans for 5 minutes. Turn onto a wire rack to cool completely. Frost with your favorite low-fat frosting.

SERVES 10

Approx Per Serving: Cal 212; Prot 3 g; Carbo 35 g; T Fat 7 g; 30% Calories from Fat; Chol <1 mg; Fiber 1 g; Sod 231 mg

Lite and Luscious Brownies

Don't let this recipe fool you. It's easy, tender, delicious, AND low in fat. Try baking them in your microwave—you'll be happily surprised! Cover with plastic wrap to keep fresh.

1/4 cup plus 2 tablespoons reduced-fat margarine or butter
2/3 cup sugar
1/2 cup egg substitute (equals 2 eggs)
1 teaspoon vanilla extract
3/4 cup flour
1/2 teaspoon baking powder
1/4 teaspoon salt
3 tablespoons baking cocoa
1/3 cup fat-free sour cream

Microwave Method:

1. Cream the margarine and sugar in a mixer bowl until light and fluffy. Add the egg substitute and vanilla, beating well.
2. Mix the flour, baking powder, salt and baking cocoa together. Stir into the creamed mixture. Fold in the sour cream.
3. Pour into a round 8-inch glass dish sprayed with nonstick vegetable cooking spray. Place on a microwave-safe rack or inverted saucer in the microwave.
4. Microwave on Medium-High (70%) for 5 1/2 to 6 1/2 minutes or until a wooden pick inserted near the center comes out clean. Let stand for 10 minutes.
5. Garnish with confectioners' sugar. Cut into wedges to serve.

Conventional Method:

1. Prepare the batter following Microwave Method Steps 1 and 2.
2. Pour into a round 8-inch baking pan sprayed with nonstick vegetable cooking spray.
3. Bake at 350 degrees for 20 to 25 minutes or until a wooden pick inserted near the center comes out clean. Let stand for 10 minutes.
4. Garnish with confectioners' sugar. Cut into wedges to serve.

Serves 10

Approx Per Serving: Cal 139; Prot 3 g; Carbo 23 g; T Fat 4 g; 27% Calories from Fat; Chol <1 mg; Fiber 1 g; Sod 183 mg

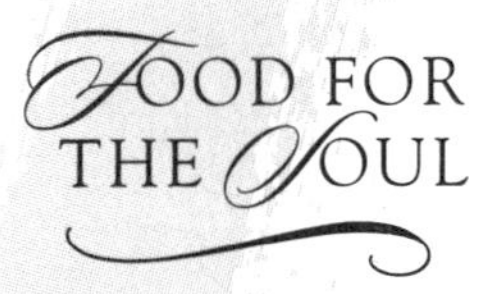

The person who has never made a mistake has never tried. No one is wrong all the time. Even a clock that has stopped is right twice a day.

COMEDY IS SIMPLY A FUNNY WAY OF BEING SERIOUS.

—Peter Ustinov

MOM'S APPLE PIE, EN CONCERT

Welcome home! There is nothing more comforting than the aroma of a pie in the oven, whether we've just walked in the door or we're watching the news. Thanks to the new prepared foods and en concert baking, we can enjoy the same goodness in half the time, with a few less fat grams and calories. It's baked in less than 30 minutes. This en concert technique works well for all double-crust pies. See the Lemon Meringue Pie recipe (page 144) for single-crust pies.

2 all ready pie pastries or All-Purpose Pie Crust (page 145)
1 cup sugar
1 teaspoon ground cinnamon
1 tablespoon flour
5 medium apples, peeled, thinly sliced
2 teaspoons reduced-fat margarine
1 teaspoon skim milk
1 teaspoon sugar

EN CONCERT METHOD:

1. Line a 9-inch glass pie plate with one pie pastry, pressing down gently to fit.
2. Combine 1 cup sugar, cinnamon and flour in a large bowl. Add the sliced apples, tossing to coat. Spoon the apples into the prepared pie plate. (Do not mound the apples in the center.) Dot with the margarine.
3. Top with the remaining pie pastry, fluting edge and cutting slits to vent. (It's fun to use family members' initials when making the slits.)
4. Brush with the milk and sprinkle with 1 teaspoon sugar.
5. Microwave on High (100%) for 8 minutes, turning once. Remove to the conventional oven.
6. Bake at 425 degrees for 15 minutes or until golden brown. Cool on a wire rack. Serve warm or cold.

SERVES 8

Approx Per Serving: Cal 392; Prot 1 g; Carbo 62 g; T Fat 16 g; 36% Calories from Fat; Chol 15 mg; Fiber 2 g; Sod 286 mg

Cinnamon Baked Apples

Apples in their infinite variety are in season all year round now. This traditional dessert shows one of the most popular recipes. It's best served warm with a dollop of whipped topping.

4 apples, cored, sliced into halves
2 tablespoons brown sugar
1/4 cup raisins
1 tablespoon red hot cinnamon candies
1 envelope whipped topping mix

Microwave Method:

1. Arrange the apple halves cored side up in an 8-inch microwave-safe dish.
2. Sprinkle the brown sugar, raisins and candies in the center of each apple.
3. Cover with plastic wrap, venting one corner.
4. Microwave on High for 4 to 5 minutes or until the apples are tender.
5. Prepare the whipped topping using package directions, substituting skim milk for whole milk.
6. Serve the apples warm with a dollop of whipped topping.

Conventional Method:

1. Arrange the apple halves cored side up in an 8-inch baking dish.
2. Sprinkle the brown sugar, raisins and candies in the center of each apple. Cover with foil.
3. Bake at 350 degrees for 25 to 30 minutes or until tender.
4. Prepare whipped topping and serve following Microwave Method Steps 5 and 6.

Serves 4

Approx Per Serving: Cal 194; Prot 1 g; Carbo 43 g; T Fat 4 g; 16% Calories from Fat; Chol 0 mg; Fiber 4 g; Sod 21 mg

Laughter eases tension and helps us find the best solution. Laugh today!

Blueberry-Peach Crisp

Raise the checkered flag! This dynamic duo is a delicious version of grandma's apple crisp. A summertime treat when all of the fruit is ripe off the vine. Micro-cook it for a warm treat and a cool kitchen.

4 peaches, peeled, sliced
2 cups fresh blueberries, rinsed, drained
1/2 cup packed brown sugar
1/2 cup each flour and rolled oats
1/2 teaspoon nutmeg
3/4 teaspoon ground cinnamon
2 tablespoons reduced-fat butter
1 envelope whipped topping mix (optional)

MICROWAVE METHOD:

1. Combine the peaches and blueberries in a shallow 9-inch microwave-safe dish.
2. Mix the brown sugar, flour, oats, nutmeg and cinnamon in a bowl. Cut in the butter until the mixture is crumbly. Sprinkle over the fruit. Cover with plastic wrap, venting one corner.
3. Microwave on High (100%) for 4 minutes; turn. Microwave for 4 to 6 minutes longer or until bubbly. Remove the plastic wrap and cover with foil. Let stand for 10 minutes.
4. Prepare the whipped topping using package directions, substituting skim milk for whole milk.
5. Serve warm or cold in individual dessert dishes with a dollop of whipped topping.

CONVENTIONAL METHOD:

1. Combine the fruit in a 9-inch baking dish. Prepare the oat topping and sprinkle over fruit following Microwave Method Step 2. Cover with foil.
2. Bake at 375 degrees for 25 to 30 minutes. Prepare whipped topping and serve following Microwave Method Steps 5 and 6.

SERVES 6

Approx Per Serving: Cal 249; Prot 4 g; Carbo 50 g; T Fat 4 g; 14% Calories from Fat; Chol 7 mg; Fiber 4 g; Sod 44 mg

Tip: *To peel peaches easily, drop into a saucepan of boiling water for 30 seconds. Remove and rub off the skin, then slice.*

MIRACLES ARE OF ALL SIZES. AND IF YOU START BELIEVING IN LITTLE MIRACLES, YOU CAN WORK UP TO THE BIGGER ONES!

—*Peale Center Plus Magazine*

Blueberry Tapioca Pudding

If you have never made pudding in the microwave, now is the time to try. (I haven't made pie filling or pudding in any other way for 15 years!) It is SO EASY with no mess or double boiler pans to clean up. Just be sure to stir from the outside edge to the middle twice during cooking and once when finished.

1 (3-ounce) package tapioca pudding mix
2 cups skim milk
1/2 cup fresh blueberries, rinsed, drained

Microwave Method:

1. Mix the pudding mix and the milk in a 4-cup glass measure.
2. Microwave on High (100%) for 6 to 8 minutes, stirring twice during cooking.
3. Stir and let cool slightly. Fold in the blueberries.
4. Chill, covered, until serving time. Spoon into stemmed dessert dishes. Garnish with fresh berries and a sprig of mint.

Conventional Method:

1. Prepare the pudding mix using package directions using 2 cups skim milk. Let cool slightly.
2. Fold in the blueberries.
3. Chill, covered, until serving time. Spoon into stemmed dessert dishes. Garnish with fresh berries and a sprig of mint.

Serves 6

Approx Per Serving: Cal 92; Prot 3 g; Carbo 20 g; T Fat <1 g; 2% Calories from Fat; Chol 1 mg; Fiber <1 g; Sod 116 mg

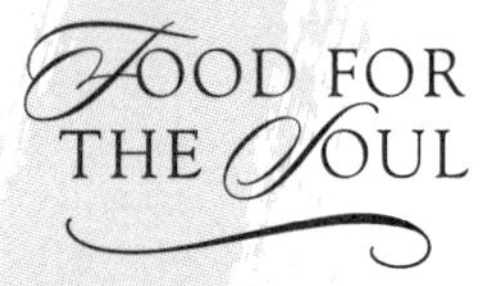

Consider the postage stamp: its usefulness consists in the ability to stick to one thing until it gets there!

—Josh Billings

DISCOVERING THAT YOU DON'T HAVE TO DO EVERYTHING CAN BE ONE OF THE GREATEST LIBERTIES OF ALL. BE GOOD IN WHAT YOU DECIDE TO DO.

—Anonymous

CHERRIES JUBILEE

Enjoy treating your guests to this grand finalé; it's spectacular, elegant and simple to prepare. Be sure to have long matches and a chafing dish. Dim the lights and enjoy the show.

6 scoops low-fat French vanilla ice cream
1 (16-ounce) can pitted Bing cherries
1 tablespoon cornstarch
1 tablespoon sugar
3 or 4 strips fresh orange peel
1 tablespoon lemon juice
1 cup brandy

MICROWAVE METHOD:

1. Place the scoops of ice cream on a plate. Freeze in the freezer until very firm. Remove to a sealable plastic bag and store in the freezer.
2. Drain the cherries, reserving the juice. Mix the cornstarch and sugar in a medium microwave-safe dish. Stir in the reserved cherry juice and orange peel.
3. Microwave on High (100%) for 3 minutes or until thickened. Add the cherries and lemon juice. Pour into a chafing dish or heat-proof dish. Microwave the brandy on High (100%) in a 2-cup glass measure for 1 minute.
4. Remove the ice cream from the freezer and place in individual dessert dishes.
5. Pour the brandy over the cherry mixture; do not stir. Dim the lights and ignite the cherries with a long match. Spoon the flaming sauce over the ice cream.

CONVENTIONAL METHOD:

1. Follow Microwave Method Steps 1 and 2, mixing in a medium saucepan.
2. Cook over medium heat until thickened, stirring constantly. Add the cherries and lemon juice. Pour into a chafing dish.
3. Heat the brandy in a small saucepan just until warm. Finish with Microwave Method Steps 4 and 5.

SERVES 6

Approx Per Serving: Cal 256; Prot 3 g; Carbo 37 g; T Fat 2 g; 7% Calories from Fat; Chol 5 mg; Fiber 2 g; Sod 49 mg

Cranberry-Apple Crisp

Cranberries add their sparkling color and their sweet-tart taste to this ever-popular American dessert. Put it together and bake while you are eating dinner. This recipe has been adapted from the microwave cookbook, Living the Good Life *by Mary Carlson, R.D., and Dottie Cramer.*

1 cup chopped fresh cranberries
1/2 cup sugar
4 cups sliced peeled apples
1 teaspoon lemon juice
2 tablespoons reduced-fat margarine
1/3 cup flour
1 cup quick-cooking oats
1/3 cup packed brown sugar
1 teaspoon ground cinnamon
1 envelope whipped topping mix

Microwave Method:

1. Combine the cranberries and sugar in a large bowl. Add the apple and lemon juice, tossing to mix. Spoon into a round 9-inch microwave-safe dish.
2. Melt the margarine in a small glass bowl in the microwave for 1 minute.
3. Add the flour, oats, brown sugar and cinnamon, stirring until crumbly. Sprinkle evenly over the cranberry mixture. Cover with plastic wrap, venting one corner.
4. Microwave on High (100%) for 8 to 10 minutes or until tender.
5. Prepare the whipped topping using package directions, substituting skim milk for whole milk. Spoon over the dessert. Serve warm.

Conventional Method:

1. Assemble the ingredients following Microwave Method Steps 1, 2 and 3, using a round 9-inch baking pan and covering with foil.
2. Bake at 350 degrees for 25 to 30 minutes.
3. Prepare topping and serve following Microwave Method Step 5.

Serves 6

Approx Per Serving: Cal 304; Prot 4 g; Carbo 61 g; T Fat 6 g; 17% Calories from Fat; Chol <1 mg; Fiber 4 g; Sod 67 mg

First we have to believe, and then we believe.

—G.C. Lichtenberg

Start your morning with the affirmation: "I believe, I believe, I believe!" Then go on to say what you believe in. Say it with gusto! You will be amazed at how positively it will affect you.

—Norman Vincent Peale

A RETENTIVE MEMORY MAY BE A GOOD THING, BUT THE ABILITY TO FORGET IS THE TRUE TOKEN OF GREATNESS.

—Elbert Hubbard

LEMON MERINGUE PIE

Light and luscious lemon meringue pie baked in less than 10 minutes!

$1\frac{1}{2}$ cups sugar
$\frac{1}{3}$ cup cornstarch
$1\frac{1}{2}$ cups water
3 egg yolks, lightly beaten
3 tablespoons butter
$\frac{1}{4}$ cup lemon juice
1 tablespoon grated lemon peel
$\frac{1}{2}$ teaspoon lemon extract
3 egg whites
$\frac{1}{4}$ teaspoon cream of tartar
6 tablespoons sugar
1 baked (9-inch) pie crust or All-Purpose Pie Crust (page 145)

EN CONCERT METHOD:

1. Combine $1\frac{1}{2}$ cups sugar with the cornstarch and water in a large glass bowl. Microwave on High (100%) for 4 to 5 minutes, stirring every 60 seconds until the mixture thickens and boils.
2. Pour a small amount of the hot mixture into the beaten egg yolks, whisking briskly. Pour the egg yolk mixture into the hot mixture, whisking constantly.
3. Microwave on High (100%) for 30 to 45 seconds. Stir in the butter, lemon juice, lemon peel and lemon extract. Pour into the baked crust.
4. Place the egg whites in a 4-cup glass measure. Microwave on High (100%) for 12 seconds to bring to room temperature.
5. Beat at medium speed until frothy. Add the cream of tartar. Add the sugar gradually 2 tablespoons at a time, beating at high speed until stiff peaks form.
6. Spread the meringue over the lemon filling, sealing to the edge.
7. Bake at 425 degrees in a conventional oven for 2 to 4 minutes or until peaks are golden.

SERVES 8

Approx Per Serving: Cal 357; Prot 3 g; Carbo 61 g; T Fat 12 g; 29% Calories from Fat; Chol 91 mg; Fiber <1 g; Sod 170 mg

All-Purpose Pie Crust

$2^1/_4$ cups flour
1 teaspoon salt
$^3/_4$ cup shortening
5 tablespoons ice water

Method:

1. Mix the flour and salt in a bowl. Cut in the shortening until the mixture forms crumbs the size of peas.
2. Place the ice water in a small bowl. Add $^1/_3$ cup of the crumb mixture to the ice water and mix well with a fork. Add to the remaining crumbs, stirring to form a dough. Chill for 30 minutes or longer.
3. Divide the dough into 2 equal portions and shape each into a flat round. Use immediately or wrap tightly with plastic wrap and freeze until needed. To use place 1 round at a time between 2 pieces of waxed paper and roll into a 10-inch circle.

Single Crust:

1. Remove the waxed paper gently from one circle and fit the pie pastry into a 9-inch pie plate. Trim and flute the edge and prick all over with a fork.
2. Bake at 425 degrees for 8 to 12 minutes or until golden brown.

Double Crust:

1. Remove the waxed paper gently from 1 circle and fit the pastry into a 9-inch pie plate. Fill as desired. Place the remaining circle on top, fluting the edge and cutting vents in the top.
2. Microwave on High (100%) for 8 to 10 minutes.
3. Bake at 425 degrees in a conventional oven for 12 to 15 minutes or until golden brown.

Yields 2 (10-inch) pastry circles

A good cook is like a sorceress who dispenses happiness.

—Elsa Schiaparelli

ENDURANCE IS NOT JUST THE ABILITY TO BEAR A HARD THING, BUT TO TURN IT INTO GLORY.

—*Philip Yancey*

FRESH PEACH MELBA

This elegant little dessert is a real treat. It is very versatile, as it is simply marvelous with raspberry purée (page 133) or chocolate sauce (page 131 or page 155), or fresh berries.

1½ cups sugar
¾ cup water
4 large fresh peaches
1 (6-ounce) container fresh raspberries
3 tablespoons sugar
1 quart fat-free frozen vanilla yogurt

METHOD:

1. Mix 1½ cups sugar with the water in a shallow 2-quart glass dish; cover with plastic wrap.
2. Microwave on High (100%) for 3 to 5 minutes or until the mixture begins to boil and thicken; stir.
3. Peel the peaches and cut into quarters. Place in the hot syrup.
4. Microwave on High (100%) for 2 to 3 minutes or until the peaches are tender.
5. Remove the peaches from the syrup to a bowl. Chill, covered, in the refrigerator.
6. Mash the raspberries with 3 tablespoons sugar in a small bowl. Cover until serving time.
7. Scoop the frozen yogurt into individual serving bowls. Top with the peaches and raspberries.

SERVES 6

Approx Per Serving: Cal 387; Prot 7 g; Carbo 92 g; T Fat <1 g; 1% Calories from Fat; Chol 2 mg; Fiber 3 g; Sod 86 mg

Tip: *If using frozen sliced peaches (4 cups), thaw completely and drain off excess liquid. If using frozen raspberries, select whole berries.*

Raspberry-Blueberry Whip

Simply elegant and guiltless. This divine dessert will satisfy even the sweetest sweet tooth. Sliced fresh strawberries are delicious in this recipe, too. Relish!

- 1 cup fresh blueberries
- 1 (6-ounce) container fresh raspberries
- 2 tablespoons confectioners' sugar
- 1 envelope whipped topping mix

Method:

1. Rinse the berries and drain in a colander. Pour into a medium bowl.
2. Combine the confectioners' sugar and whipped topping mix in a bowl. Prepare the whipped topping using package directions, substituting skim milk for whole milk.
3. Fold the topping mixture into the berries. Spoon into individual dessert dishes.
4. Garnish with a sprig of fresh mint.

Serves 6

Approx Per Serving: Cal 81; Prot 1 g; Carbo 15 g; T Fat 2 g; 17% Calories from Fat; Chol <1 mg; Fiber 3 g; Sod 12 mg

Attitude is everything—if we monitor our attitude, we will find we can have both endurance and find glory.

You are young at any age if you are planning for tomorrow.

—*The Sword of the Lord*

Instant Strawberry Cake

Here's some fun for the kids. This is a great project for a rainy day. Of course, it's not just for kids to make—well, we all still have some kid in us—right? It's ready to eat warm in less than twenty minutes, and yes, it tastes good, too! May substitute your favorite gelatin flavor for the strawberry gelatin.

1 (7 1/2-ounce) jar pear and pineapple Junior baby food
1 (3-ounce) package strawberry gelatin
1 (1-layer) package yellow cake mix

Microwave Method:

1. Mix the baby food and gelatin in a bowl until smooth. Pour evenly into a round 9-inch glass dish.
2. Prepare the cake mix using package directions, substituting egg substitute for whole eggs. Pour evenly over the gelatin mixture.
3. Microwave on Medium-High (70%) for 6 to 7 minutes or until a wooden pick inserted near the center comes out clean, turning once during cooking.
4. Let stand for 5 to 10 minutes. Garnish with confectioners' sugar before serving.

Conventional Method:

1. Mix the baby food and gelatin in a bowl until smooth. Pour evenly into a round 9-inch cake pan sprayed with nonstick vegetable cooking spray.
2. Prepare the cake mix using package directions, substituting egg substitute for whole eggs. Pour evenly over the gelatin mixture.
3. Bake at 350 degrees for 20 minutes or until a wooden pick inserted near the center comes out clean. Cool in the pan on a wire rack for 5 to 10 minutes. Garnish with confectioners' sugar before serving.

Serves 8

Approx Per Serving: Cal 427; Prot 6 g; Carbo 65 g; T Fat 16 g; 34% Calories from Fat; Chol <1 mg; Fiber 1 g; Sod 515 mg

Passionate Strawberries

Be sure to select the biggest and best quality strawberries that you can find for this deliciously sensual and easy dessert. Make them a few hours to one day ahead. Keep lightly covered with foil in the refrigerator.

12 large strawberries
1 (12-ounce) package semisweet chocolate chips
2 teaspoons shortening

Microwave Method:

1. Rinse the strawberries and pat dry with paper towels. Do not remove the stems.
2. Combine the chocolate chips and shortening in a 4-cup glass measure.
3. Microwave on Medium-High (70%) in the center of the microwave for 1 1/2 minutes; stir well. Microwave for 30 to 60 seconds longer. (Chocolate chips will look glossy and soft but not melted.) Stir gently until smooth, but do not overstir!
4. Swirl each strawberry gently in the chocolate mixture to cover 2/3 of the berry.
5. Place on a waxed-paper-lined tray. Chill for 45 minutes or until the chocolate has hardened.
6. Store in the refrigerator in a square 8-inch dish covered with foil until ready to serve. Garnish with mint sprigs to serve.

Conventional Method:

1. Rinse the strawberries and pat dry with paper towels. Do not remove the stems.
2. Combine the chocolate chips and shortening in the top of a double boiler. Cook over medium heat until the chocolate is melted, stirring frequently.
3. Follow Microwave Method Steps 4, 5 and 6 to assemble and serve.

Serves 4

Approx Per Serving: Cal 442; Prot 4 g; Carbo 57 g; T Fat 28 g; 51% Calories from Fat; Chol 0 mg; Fiber 6 g; Sod 10 mg

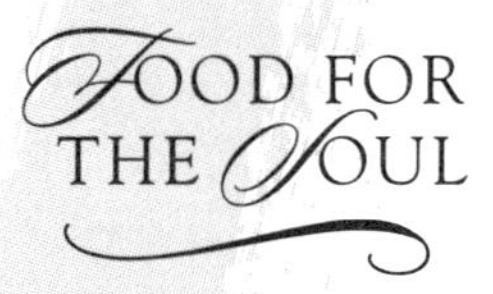

Respect your body and keep it healthy! Revel in feeding and nourishing it with exercise and good food. It will reward you graciously!

Food for the Soul

We nourish the soul when we find value in the stillness of the moment, recognizing that the present time is the only time there is.

—*Gerald Jampolsky, M.D.*

Strawberry-Tapioca Swirl

This pudding is easy to mix up at the beginning of your meal preparation, or cook it while you're watching TV the night before. You may use prepared tapioca purchased from a deli, but it will have lots more calories!

1 (3-ounce) package tapioca pudding mix
2 cups skim milk
1 (6-ounce) jar strawberry jelly

Microwave Method:

1. Combine the tapioca pudding mix and milk in a glass bowl.
2. Microwave on High (100%) for 5 to 7 minutes or until thickened, stirring twice during cooking.
3. Chill, covered, for 2 hours or until firm.
4. Alternate layers of the tapioca and strawberry jelly in individual dessert dishes to serve.

Conventional Method:

1. Prepare the pudding mix in a 1½-quart saucepan using package directions, substituting 2 cups skim milk for whole milk.
2. Chill, covered, for 2 hours or until firm.
3. Alternate layers of the tapioca and strawberry jelly in individual dessert dishes to serve.

Serves 4

Approx Per Serving: Cal 255; Prot 4 g; Carbo 57 g; T Fat <1 g; 1% Calories from Fat; Chol 2 mg; Fiber <1 g; Sod 194 mg

Sweet Ambrosia

Sweet Ambrosia has a mélange of meanings—"food of the Greek and Roman gods," "something sweet and extremely pleasant to taste." Enjoy this light and satisfying dessert—it just may replenish your soul, as Carole King wrote in her popular song, Ambrosia.

1 (16-ounce) can fruit cocktail, drained
1 (16-ounce) can pineapple chunks, drained
1 unpeeled apple, chopped
1 cup miniature marshmallows
1 teaspoon Grand Marnier liqueur (optional)
1/4 cup flaked coconut, toasted

Method:

1. Combine the fruit cocktail, pineapple, apple, marshmallows and Grand Marnier in a large bowl, tossing to mix. Chill in the refrigerator until serving time.
2. Stir in the coconut. Spoon into individual dessert dishes. Garnish with maraschino cherries.

Serves 6

Approx Per Serving: Cal 136; Prot 1 g; Carbo 33 g; T Fat 1 g; 8% Calories from Fat; Chol 0 mg; Fiber 2 g; Sod 10 mg

Tip: *Toast the coconut in the microwave. Place in a glass pie plate. Microwave on High (100%) for 2 to 3 minutes or until golden brown, stirring once or twice during cooking. Store in a plastic bag or a covered container.*

It is a well-adjusted person who makes the same mistake twice without getting nervous!

—Jane Heard

You can have anything you want if you want it desperately enough. You must want it with an exuberance that erupts through the skin and joins the energy that created the world.

—*Sheila Graham*

Fruit Kabobs with Chocolate Dip

This is an easy and entertaining way to serve dessert. Just put out the pretty platter of fruit, 6-inch wooden kabob skewers, and warm chocolate sauce. Let your guests select their own luscious medley!

2 medium ripe pears, cored, cut into 8 wedges each
2 ripe nectarines, cut into 8 wedges each
16 grapefruit sections
2 kiwifruit, peeled, cut into 6 wedges each
16 large strawberries
2 bananas, cut into 1/2-inch slices
30 seedless green grapes
Juice of 1 large lemon (about 3 tablespoons)
Chocolate Dip (page 153)

Method:

1. Arrange the fruit attractively on a pretty platter. Brush with lemon juice. Chill, covered, until serving time.
2. Have the guests skewer the fruit onto 6-inch wooden skewers and dip in the warm Chocolate Dip.

Serves 16

Approx Per Serving: Cal 90; Prot 1 g; Carbo 22 g; T Fat 1 g; 6% Calories from Fat; Chol 0 mg; Fiber 3 g; Sod 22 mg

Chocolate Dip

This is so delicious, you'd never guess it contains so few fat grams! Be sure to serve it warm. To heat up the sauce, microwave on Medium-High (70%) for 20 to 30 seconds.

1 1/2 cups sugar
2/3 cup baking cocoa
2 tablespoons cornstarch
1 1/2 cups water
1 tablespoon reduced-fat margarine
1 teaspoon vanilla extract

Microwave Method:

1. Combine the sugar, baking cocoa and cornstarch in a 4-cup glass measure. Add the water gradually, stirring well.
2. Microwave on Medium-High (70%) for 2 1/2 to 3 minutes or until the mixture begins to boil, stirring every 60 seconds. Stir in the margarine and vanilla until smooth.
3. Serve warm in a pretty shallow dish.

Conventional Method:

1. Combine the sugar, baking cocoa and cornstarch in a 1 1/2-quart saucepan. Add the water gradually, stirring well.
2. Cook over medium heat for 3 to 4 minutes or until the mixture comes to a boil, stirring constantly. Remove from the heat. Stir in the margarine and vanilla until smooth.
3. Serve warm in a pretty shallow dish.

Yields 2 cups

Approx Per Serving: Cal 45; Prot <1 g; Carbo 11 g; T Fat <1 g; 6% Calories from Fat; Chol 0 mg; Fiber 1 g; Sod 2 mg

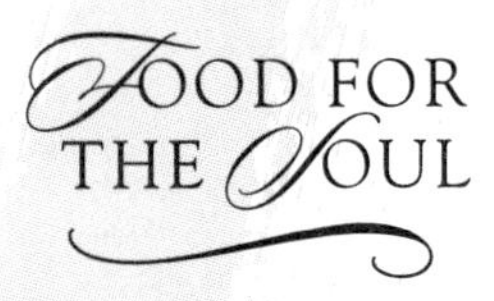

To handle yourself, use your head. To handle others, use your heart. The best way to succeed in life is to act on the advise you give others!

—Anonymous

WAIKIKI SUNDAES

Scoops of creamy low-fat frozen French vanilla yogurt, quick tropical sauce, and a sprinkling of toasted coconut—you'll never dream this grand finalé is low in fat.

1/3 cup flaked coconut
1/4 ripe banana
1 1/2 teaspoons lemon juice
1/2 cup pineapple-orange marmalade
1/2 cup apricot preserves
1/8 teaspoon rum or almond extract
1 quart low-fat frozen French vanilla yogurt

METHOD:

1. Spread the coconut evenly in a round shallow dish.
2. Microwave on High (100%) for 1 1/2 to 2 1/2 minutes or until the flakes are toasted, stirring twice from the outside edge to the middle. Set aside.
3. Mash the banana with the lemon juice in a 4-cup glass measure. Stir in the marmalade and preserves.
4. Microwave on High (100%) for 2 to 3 minutes, stirring once during cooking. Stir in the rum extract.
5. Scoop the frozen yogurt into individual serving dishes. Spoon the sauce over the yogurt. Sprinkle with the toasted coconut. Garnish with maraschino cherries with stems. Serve immediately.

SERVES 8

Approx Per Serving: Cal 219; Prot 5 g; Carbo 47 g; T Fat 2 g; 9% Calories from Fat; Chol 5 mg; Fiber <1 g; Sod 81 mg

CHARACTER CONTRIBUTES TO BEAUTY. IT FORTIFIES A WOMAN AS HER YOUTH FADES. A MODE OF CONDUCT, A STANDARD OF COURAGE, DISCIPLINE, FORTITUDE, AND INTEGRITY CAN DO A GREAT DEAL TO MAKE A WOMAN BEAUTIFUL.

—Jacqueline Bisset

Light Chocolate Sauce in a Jiffy

Chocolaty, velvety, and low in fat. Serve over frozen yogurt, fresh fruit, or angel food cake. May store leftover sauce in a covered container in the refrigerator. Reheat in the microwave on Medium-High (70%) at 20-second intervals until heated through, stirring well.

1/2 cup sugar
3 1/2 tablespoons baking cocoa
1 1/2 tablespoons cornstarch
1/8 teaspoon salt
1/2 cup water
2 teaspoons reduced-fat margarine or butter
1 teaspoon vanilla extract

MICROWAVE METHOD:

1. Combine the sugar, baking cocoa, cornstarch and salt in a 2-cup glass measure. Stir in the water until smooth.
2. Microwave on High (100%) for 2 minutes, stirring twice during cooking. Add the margarine.
3. Microwave for 15 seconds longer. Stir in the vanilla.

CONVENTIONAL METHOD:

1. Combine the sugar, baking cocoa, cornstarch and salt in a 1-quart saucepan. Stir in the water until smooth.
2. Cook over medium heat until the mixture begins to thicken, stirring frequently; reduce the heat to low. Add the margarine.
3. Cook for 1 to 2 minutes or until thick and creamy, stirring constantly. Stir in the vanilla.

SERVES 6

Approx Per Serving: Cal 86; Prot 1 g; Carbo 20 g; T Fat 1 g; 8% Calories from Fat; Chol 0 mg; Fiber 1 g; Sod 57 mg

MAKE AN INVENTORY OF YOUR JOYS. TO IMPROVE YOURSELF, DO NOT DISCOUNT THE IMPORTANCE OF CULTIVATING JOY. MANY ATHLETIC COACHES TRAIN THE BEGINNER IN TENNIS, GOLF, AND OTHER SPORTS BY DIRECTING THEM TO SING AS THEY PLAY. IT HAS THE EFFECT OF UNLOCKING THE MUSCLES. SING!

THE EDITORS HAVE ATTEMPTED TO PRESENT THESE FAMILY RECIPES IN A FORM THAT ALLOWS APPROXIMATE NUTRITIONAL VALUES TO BE COMPUTED. PERSONS WITH DIETARY OR HEALTH PROBLEMS OR WHOSE DIETS REQUIRE CLOSE MONITORING SHOULD NOT RELY SOLELY ON THE NUTRITIONAL INFORMATION PROVIDED. THEY SHOULD CONSULT THEIR PHYSICIANS OR A REGISTERED DIETITIAN FOR SPECIFIC INFORMATION.

NUTRITIONAL PROFILE GUIDELINES

Nutritional information for these recipes is computed from information derived from many sources, including materials supplied by the United States Department of Agriculture, computer databanks and journals in which the information is assumed to be in the public domain. However, many specialty items, new products and processed foods may not be available from these sources or may vary from the average values used in these profiles. More information on new and/or specific products may be obtained by reading the nutrient labels. Unless otherwise specified, the nutritional profile of these recipes is based on all measurements being level.

ABBREVIATIONS FOR NUTRITIONAL PROFILE

Cal — Calories	T Fat — Total Fat	Sod — Sodium
Prot — Protein	Chol — Cholesterol	g — grams
Carbo — Carbohydrates	Fiber — Dietary Fiber	mg — milligrams

* **Alcoholic ingredients** have been analyzed for basic ingredients, although cooking causes the evaporation of alcohol, thus decreasing caloric content.
* **Sour cream** and **yogurt** are the types available commercially.
* **Cake mixes** that are prepared using package directions include 3 eggs and 1/2 cup oil.
* **Chicken**, cooked for boning and chopping, has been roasted and is skinless; this method yields the lowest caloric values.
* **Eggs** are all large.
* **Flour** is unsifted all-purpose flour.
* **Oil** is any type of vegetable cooking oil. Shortening is hydrogenated vegetable shortening.
* **Salt** and other ingredients to taste as noted in the ingredients have not been included in the nutritional profile.
* If a choice of ingredients has been given, the nutritional profile information reflects the first option. If a choice of amounts has been given, the nutritional profile reflects the greater amount.

INDEX

INDEX

NDEX

To order additional copies of

mail order to

Eating In With Joan Toole® Consulting Services
P.O. Box 937
Lake Forest, Illinois 60045

or call 847-735-0036

or send fax to 847-735-0037

or visit our website at www.cookwave.com

Be sure to include Your Name, Complete Address and Telephone Number

Make checks payable to: *Eating In Consulting Services*

If paying by credit card, include Card Number, Expiration Date and Signature

Visa, MasterCard and Discover accepted

Price per copy	$29.95
Plus postage and handling	4.50
Total per copy	$34.45

(Illinois residents add appropriate county sales tax)

For volume purchases call 847-735-0036

Allow three weeks for delivery